A Field Guide to Finding Your Self

By Dr. Corey Lee Lewis

DEDICATION

This book is dedicated to my parents, Lon and Nancy Lewis,
who instilled in me a love of nature, taught me to be my true self
and always supported me in following my dreams.

TABLE OF CONTENTS

01 | FIND YOUR SELF NOW

If you're reading this, Congratulations on Getting Lost!

I say "Congratulations!" because you have to become lost before you can be found.

Now, with this guide and your actions, you can find your self, again.

Once you find your self, the two of you can sit around the campfire shooting whisky and sharing stories of how crazy and harrowing your experience of being lost was, because that is one of the great joys of getting lost and found: once you are found, you get to reminisce, exaggerate and brag about the experience of being lost.

In fact, if you think about it, nothing makes for a better story, or makes you grow more than the experience of getting lost, or failing at something, and then getting found, or succeeding at it.

So, if you haven't ever gotten lost or felt lost, you should try it some time. I highly recommend it, if for no other reason than just so you can experience and enjoy what a great feeling it is to get found.

That's my advice to everyone: "Get Lost!" and "Get Found!" "Find Your Self Now!"

I know that many people like to joke about "finding your self," as in "How could you lose your self? You're always right here." But losing your sense of self, your feeling of who you are, losing your purpose, these are serious things. I have known people who have lost themselves in addictions or abusive relationships and it is no laughing matter. I've known people to get lost in careers or causes and it is serious business.

It doesn't matter whether you have lost your way in a natural environment, urban area, or a destructive mindset, the dangers are still very real.

I used to teach Wilderness Survival and worked on backcountry trail and forestry crews and rescue teams in some of the wildest deserts and mountains of Nevada and California. And I can tell you many stories of people getting lost and found in the most dire of circumstances: Stories of dehydration and heat stroke in the desert, of sheltering in snow caves through storms in the mountains, stories of injuries, evacuations, illnesses and starvation. In these stories getting lost meant that life and limb were literally on the line.

In fact, the most frightening story I ever experienced was when we lost my dad. We were on vacation, body surfing in Mexico, and having an amazing time. The waves were rolling into the shore in huge tubes, which we didn't know at the time, but are a sign of danger. Just moments before my dad's accident, a large wave I was body surfing on flipped me forward in a complete summersault and landed me on my butt in the sand.

As I stood in the shallow surf resting, I suddenly heard my mom scream out "Corey!" and I looked to where my dad was, just seconds before, and he was gone. I waded out into the water and began searching for him in the crashing surf, but there was no sign of him. I couldn't see through the foaming water and breaking waves, so I was feeling around blindly, hoping to bump into him with my feet or hands. I had visions running through my mind of his body being towed out to sea by the current and never found.

Then, after an agonizing amount of time, I saw his hand underneath the waves and grabbed it. When I pulled him to the surface, I could see by the glazed eyes and locked jaw that he was already gone. The doctors at the hospital later told us that he died the instant his neck was broken, when the powerful wave drove him headfirst into the sand.

I pulled him through the surf and up onto the shore and began chest compressions while my wife began rescue breathing. The entire time I knew that he was already gone, that he was lost to us, but I was determined to bring him back. We continued with CPR for minutes, until finally, he sputtered and breathed, and his eyes opened and I knew he had come back to us. He made a full recovery and today he is healthy and happy and continuing to live a purposeful life.

For all of those agonizing minutes, I knew that if we continued with CPR there was only a very slim chance we could bring him back to life. But, I also knew that if we stopped trying, he would be gone forever. His life was literally on the line.

FIELD NOTES

We are defined by our actions not our intentions.

And powerful actions come from powerful decisions.

So, the first action you must take, right now, is to make a powerful decision that you will take action on the ideas in this book.

And just so you know, life and limb are always on the line. Even right now. Even for you.

Your life literally depends upon whether you find your self or remain lost. Whether you will be happy and fulfilled during your remaining years, whether you will achieve and experience those things you dream of, literally depends on you Finding Your Self, discovering your purpose, your direction and following it.

What greater purpose do you have in life than finding and pursuing your purpose?

How can you find your self and your purpose unless you choose a direction?

It doesn't matter whether you are lost in a desert, jungle or mountain wilderness, or in the wilderness of daily life, Right Now your entire life is on the line.

The two key parts of that sentence are: "Now" and "Your."

"Now:"

Now is the time to make a change, to do something different. Not tomorrow, not next year, right now. Today is the day to begin.

"Your:"

It's your life, no one else's. It's all up to you, and nobody else can do it or decide for you, and there are no "shoulds" or "should nots." There are only "Dos" and "Don'ts." Because you are the only one who can decide what you want and the only one who can do it.

It doesn't matter what other people think you "should" or "shouldn't" do. The only thing that matters is what you want to "Do" and "Don't" want to do. So, don't waste any time "shoulding" on your self, or worrying about what others will think. This is your journey and you are the only one on it, so trust in your self that you know what is right for you. You will know the right direction to go in, the right course of action to take, when it appears before you.

Whether you are lost and alone in a mountain wilderness or the wilderness of your life, there comes a moment when you must say "Now" is the time to take decisive action, and in this moment it is "Your" decision, and nobody else's, about what action to take.

This is exactly where you stand now, looking around, trying to get your bearings, reviewing the landscape of your past experiences in life, trying to guess at the weather as you look to your future. I know exactly where you stand. I understand because I've stood there before.

I have helped find and rescue people who were lost in the wilderness (both real and metaphorical) and I have been lost many times myself, and each time I have found myself again. So, I would like to offer this book as a guide to help you find your self again.

The truth is that there is nothing wrong with getting lost because it happens all the time in life. I have been lost in all kinds of places like shopping malls and parking lots, in high school, in a career, in relationships, in alcohol, in causes and competitions and all kinds of different things. So, I have quite a bit of experience finding my self, and I have succeeded in doing it again, and again, and again.

You see, as you grow and change, "your self," also changes, and sometimes you change so much that you don't recognize your self anymore and then, you are indeed lost.

Since you, like me, were wise enough to go and get lost, I will share with you in this Field Guide a few of the ways I have discovered to Find Your Self again.

Now, before we begin (which we already have) let me tell you about this Field Guide and suggest a few different ways in which you might use it.

Each short chapter of the Field Guide will prescribe an action for you to take and explain why that action is beneficial and will often include stories of those who have undertaken the same action (people like me or my coaching clients and seminar participants). Although I have left spaces for you to write out your answers to the various exercises in this Field Guide, you will also want a journal or something to write in as you complete the exercises in the Field Guide, to record and reflect on your experiences.

After you read each chapter and complete the action prescribed, you can turn to the map in the back of the Field Guide to record your new insights about your self there. In this way, by the time you finish reading and taking action on the ideas in this book, you will have a map to find your self that you created all by your self.

You may use this Field Guide in any way that suits you. As long as you realize that this is called a "Field Guide" because it's about you getting out there and taking action.

This is not a book to simply read and enjoy. This is a catalyst designed to spur you on to taking many different new actions in your life. So, you can read the Field Guide in any way you like, as long as you take action and find your self.

You might make a powerful decision that as you read the *Field Guide to Finding Your Self* you will perform each Action in order, immediately after having read that section.

Or you might make a powerful decision that as you read the *Field Guide to Finding Your Self* you will perform those Actions you are most attracted to in any order that you want.

Or you might make a powerful decision to read the entire *Field*

Guide to Finding Your Self and then to re-read and perform all, or some, of the Actions described.

Regardless of how you choose to read and use the *Field Guide to Finding Your Self* I urge you to make sure you Take Action, and actually perform the activities described, and that you make sure to complete at least Three of those Actions which you feel the most resistant to doing.

We are defined by our actions not our intentions.

So, if you are going to be successful in finding your self, or defining your self, then you must take powerful action.

And powerful actions come from powerful decisions.

So, the first action you must take, right now, is to make a powerful decision that you will take action on the ideas in this book.

Go ahead, take all the time you need to make your powerful decision.

I'll wait. I'm very patient.

Fill in your name below and repeat, out loud, the following statement of conviction:

I _____ *(your name)* am committed to taking powerful action on the ideas in this book and to use them to connect to my highest good and my truest self, so that I am living the life of my dreams every day, and experiencing and expressing the best version of myself I can imagine.

Congratulations! Now that you have made the powerful decision to take action, you have defined your self as one who takes action, and you will come to find your self in the future as someone who takes powerful action. And that is a great feeling to have, to feel confident and certain, to know that you are the type of person now who takes immediate and powerful action on your dreams and desires, and that you can count on your self to do so. This is who you are beginning to find your self to be.

Now, that you have decided to be that person, let the journey to Find Your Self begin....

02 | FIND YOUR NEXT SELF

If you ever get lost in a remote area, the mountains or desert, jungle or forest, the first thing to do, the moment you realize that you are lost is to stop and memorize the landscape where you are. This becomes your new home, or the center to which you will always return. Then take several short scouting trips to look for familiar landmarks, exploring the edges of the area you are now in. Often you will be able to recognize something and find your way back, without running the risk of becoming even more lost than you initially were. Quite often, that familiar landmark is just on the edge of the horizon, just on the edge of our perception.

When my brother and I were very young, maybe 8 and 11 years old, we got lost in the Rocky Mountains of Colorado. We were on a two week long horse packing trip with my parents and grandparents, when we awoke one morning to discover two of the horses were gone. The adults saddled up and went looking for the two escapees while my brother, Bart, and I searched closer to camp on foot. In a panic to find the missing horses we weren't paying much attention to our surroundings and soon we realized that we were standing in the middle of a trackless forest with no idea where we were or which direction it was back to camp.

Once we realized that we were lost, we began screaming for help and running around in circles like chickens with our heads cut off. I climbed a really tall tree only to find that I couldn't see a thing from inside the forest's thick canopy. Then we remembered the emergency whistles mom put around our necks on a piece of string and we began blowing with all of our might, filling the forest with their piercing sound.

As we screamed and shouted and blew our whistles, we ran about the forest frantically, darting from tree to tree, looking for anything familiar. "Oh my god, we're lost!" I wailed at Bart. "What if mom and dad can't find us?" I was crying and overcome with fear.

After exhausting ourselves completely, we sat and listened to the forest in silence for a few minutes, quickly realizing that no one heard us and no one was coming to find us. Finally Bart noticed that the forest looked a little brighter and sunnier in one direction and suggested we try that way to see if we could find our way out of it. We knew that if we could find the edge of the forest, we would be able to see the surrounding mountains and landmarks and know which way to go in order to get back to camp.

Soon, the thick pine and fir gave way to aspen and then we were out of the trees, standing in a large meadow. Immediately we could see where camp was and we went straight back and didn't leave again. When my parents returned with the errant horses, they found us sitting safely by the campfire. Unwilling to admit we had gotten lost, we just told our parents we had gotten tired and came back to camp to rest. We never shared our dirty little secret.

Once we were able to see that meadow, we knew exactly where we were and what direction we needed to go. The really funny thing is, when we were panicking and "lost" we were less than a hundred yards from the meadow. It was right next to us the entire time.

In a similar manner, when I talk to people in my coaching sessions or seminars about finding themselves or their purpose(s) in life, I find that every one of them has an idea (or several ideas) that have been hovering on the edges of their mind for quite some time: A tenuous and tentative idea, or landmark, that flits about on the edges of their awareness, like the shadow of a butterfly.

An idea about something that they might, perhaps, maybe, someday, do... Ideas like maybe I could build something with wood, or learn to dance, or sing in a choir, or start fly fishing, or write a book, or whatever.

It doesn't matter what the idea is, or how big or small, how significant or trivial. All that matters is that there is an idea that has been visiting you tentatively, whispering in your ear every now and then, and you know exactly what that idea is. You haven't ever really entertained it, or thought about it much seriously though. You haven't ever started working on it in earnest, but you have thought about it from time to time.

You know that you have at least one, if not several, ideas like this.

You probably feel a bit unsure about them, a bit hesitant or afraid. You probably wonder if they would turn out to be unpleasant and a waste of time. That's okay. Don't worry about that now. You don't have to do them yet. You still get to decide.

So, just for now, hypothetically speaking, what are some of those ideas?

These ideas have been hanging around because they have the potential to be Your Next Self, to be the Next thing you do, learn, create or enjoy.

I am sure that you, like me, have ideas you wonder about, things you toy with in your mind but they might not seem possible, or feasible.

What is it? What are they?

What is that idea that has been nagging you lately?

What is that thing you've been thinking of doing someday? What is that thing you are interested in learning about? Where do you find your mind keeps returning to? What are those things that you've been wondering "what if?" about for years?

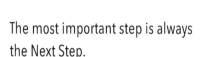

FIELD NOTES

It doesn't matter how you start. All that matters is that you begin.

The most important step is always the Next Step.

You will never know if that one idea is your next favorite hobby, or the thing you were destined to do in life, unless you begin to take action on it.

Write them down now. Go ahead and skip to the back of the chapter and write down the first few things that come to mind.

Once you have your list, pick one idea off it.

This idea is now the first direction you have decided to explore in order to find Your Next Self. Because, remember, your entire life depends on you getting found.

So, this idea, it is the direction you have decided to go in Next.

For whatever reason, you haven't explored this idea or direction yet, and that's okay. Now is the time to take action though and to see those reasons for what they are—excuses—and to let them go and just give it a shot, just go for it.

The fears you have been holding are illusions. Maybe you haven't started because you are afraid you won't succeed or that you won't like it. But these are empty fears. There is no failure here only feedback. After you take action, after you choose a direction and start exploring it, if you don't like it, then you just come back to center, back to where you started from, and pick a new direction.

Remember the strategy we discussed for finding your self in the wilderness. Memorize where you are at. Pick a few different directions to explore. Try each direction out and return to your home base if it's not a promising one. Then, try a different direction.

The same strategy applies to finding your self in the wilderness of life. Write out your list of different directions to explore. Try a direction out and if it's not a promising one, return to your list, and explore a different direction.

When I was in graduate school I decided I wanted to earn my Ph.D. and become a tenured professor and this gave me a wonderful direction and purpose to pursue. Fifteen years later, after succeeding in getting my dream job and earning tenure, I felt lost in my career, lost in the University. I remember hesitantly telling the life coach I was working with at the time, Nova Wightman, "I know it sounds crazy, but I think maybe, if it was possible, I want to do what you do. I want to leave the University and become a life coach and have time to write books."

To me it sounded crazy at first, to give up the direction I had been pursuing for fifteen years, but that is exactly what I did. She referred me to a business development coach, Dustin Vice, who I hired and the next thing I knew I was training with Dr. Richard Bandler the founder of Neuro-Linguistic Programming, opening my own practice and publishing my next book.

You don't have to be successful to start, but you have to start in order to be successful. So find some way to get started on your idea, to begin to take action.

There are many different forms of action you can take.

Perhaps you will start by reading a book or watching an instructional video online, or taking a class, or buying some tools and materials and diving right in.

It doesn't matter how you start. All that matters is that you begin.

Take that first step and see where it leads you next. Each step will lead to the next step, and they all will lead to Your Next Self.

Think about it this way: If you were going to run a marathon what would be the most important step? Some people would say it's the first step, because you can't start without taking the first step. Others might say it is the last step, because you can't finish without taking the last step. But, of course, you can't finish unless you take all the steps in between the first and last step, so they are just as important too.

This means that the correct answer is that the most important step is always the Next Step. From wherever you are, the Next Step is the most important one to take. At the end of the race the most important step is the last step, during the race it is all of the next steps, and before the race it is the first step. The most important step is always the next step from where you are now.

So, what is the next step you are going to take, to explore that idea, that direction?

Write that first step down now and take that first step today. That first step will lead you to your next step, which will lead you to others and all together they will lead you to find your next self.

Lao Tzu, the author of the *Tao Te Ching*, was famous for walking all over China, from one side of the country to the other, as he shared his teachings. Even in old age, he kept up this practice, walking thousands of miles, over mountains and plains, and through jungles and deserts. He was often asked "Old man, how do you walk so many miles?"

"That's easy," he would reply, laughing. "You just put one foot in front of the other. One foot in front of the other and you go up a mountain. One foot in front of the other and you go down a mountain. One foot in front of the other and you go through the desert. Always it is one foot in front of the other."

Now it is time for you to put one foot in front of the other and take the first step to find your next self.

As you begin exploring your new direction, or working on your new endeavor, pay attention to how it makes you feel.

Does your new hobby or interest make you feel good? Is it fun and exciting? Is it challenging and rewarding? Does it feel like it fits you and who you are, or does it feel like you will grow to fit it? Is it something you want to continue to pursue, to get even more involved in or not?

Think of this as an experiment in action, an exploration. You are going to take action by doing something you've always thought about doing as an experiment to see if you like it and then you are going to observe the results. If you like it, then do more of it. If you don't like it, then choose another idea to take experimental action on, or a different direction to explore.

You will never know if that one idea is your next favorite hobby, or the thing you were destined to do in life, unless you begin to take action on it.

You will never know if this is the direction home, unless you begin to explore it.

Finding Your Next Self
ACTIONS TO TAKE

1. Write down that one thing (or several things) that hovers on the edge of your mind, that one thing (or things) that you have been thinking about doing for a long time.

One Thing I can Do:

_____

_____

_____

_____

_____

_____

2. Write down all the different ways you could get started doing that thing or moving in that direction.

Different Steps I can take to do it:

_____

_____

_____

_____

_____

_____

_____

3. Decide on your first step and take it Today.

The first step I will take is:

_____

_____

The date on which I will take it is:

_____

_____

The Next step I will take is:

_____

_____

The date on which I will take it is:

_____

_____

The Next step I will take is:

_____

_____

The date on which I will take it is:

_____

_____

The Next step I will take is:

_____

_____

The date on which I will take it is:

_____

_____

The Next step I will take is:

_____

_____

The date on which I will take it is:

_____

_____

The Next step I will take is:

_____

_____

The date on which I will take it is:

_____

_____

(to be continued by you)

03 | FIND YOUR FUN SELF

One winter I was snowshoeing with some friends high up in the Sierras and we got lost in time, not space. We had been snowshoeing and enjoying the views all afternoon and having so much fun that we completely lost track of time. When we noticed how late it was, we immediately started back toward the trailhead. As we trudged along, I began doing the math in my head and it became clear that it was going to get dark several hours before we would make it back to our car.

This left us with several choices. We could use what remaining light was left to make a camp and settle in for the long cold night, and then find our way safely home the next day during daylight. Or, we could hurry back as fast as we could, trying to beat the darkness, and running the risk of getting injured or lost. Or, we could take our time going back, being careful not to lose the trail or get hurt, and accept the risk of hiking for several hours in the dark.

We chose the final option and decided to have fun with it and make this an enjoyable "night hike." So, with our headlamps on we hiked carefully back, paying close attention to our footing and signs of the trail along the way. Soon, we were singing a tune, laughing and making it a game to see who could spot the next footprint or trail sign first. Eventually, a half-moon rose up and cast its light on the white snow all around us, making our headlamps almost unnecessary. Eventually, we were marveling at the stars in the clear sky above and the moon shadows all around us and having one of the most enjoyable winter hikes any of us could remember.

What could have become a serious survival situation turned out to be a pleasurable experience because we didn't just focus on getting through it, we focused on enjoying it. By embracing the situation and taking the time to have fun with it and to enjoy ourselves, rather than just racing home were able to avoid potentially serious disaster.

FIELD NOTES

Regardless of whether you take one action each day, or one each week, as you do the things on your list, embrace the activity and enjoy it as much as you can while it is happening.

As adults it is very common for us to get stuck in a rut in our life. We get the career and the family, and we get so caught up in doing what has to be done, in working and shopping and cleaning and paying bills that we forget to have fun.

As an adult I've often had difficulty doing things just for fun. If it's work, I'll do it. If it has a practical purpose or will benefit others, I'm all over it. But, if it's just frivolous fun, I have often neglected to take the time to do it. I might say that I'm too busy, or I might simply not think about doing that fun thing for months. When I was younger I wasn't this way. I was all about fun and adventures, but somehow I had lost touch with that part of myself in adulthood.

My friend, Life Coach and Author Nova Wightman discusses this in her wonderful book *Awake and Aligned*. She discusses the importance of being aligned with your true self and your sources of joy, and how vitally important it is to give your self experiences of fun, relaxation, excitement and joy on a regular basis.

So, in this Find Your Fun Self exercise you are going to begin writing out a list of things that you really enjoy, things that bring you pleasure, make you happy, and are fun for you, even if, and especially if, they don't have a practical purpose.

This list might include things like watching your favorite TV show, reading a book, walking in nature, getting a pedicure, having sex, playing golf, throwing pottery, painting, writing poetry, singing, hanging out with friends, gardening, bowling, doing yoga or martial arts, cooking, dancing, seeing a play in a theater, playing with your kids, having sex, bird watching, fishing, shopping, playing music or chess, working with wood, or building models, or having sex, or whatever.

List everything and anything that you enjoy.

The longer your list, the better.

Write down things you know that you enjoy and things you haven't done in months or years. Include things you used to like doing and even add things you've never done before, but you think you might like doing.

Go ahead and start on that list right now. Write Ten things down, Write Now!

I'll wait. I'm patient.

Flip to the end of this chapter right now and get started with your list.

Great! Now that you have at least ten things written down on your Fun Self List, you've got it started. Return to your list and add to it continually, until it's as long as you can make it.

I remember a powerful experience I had with this exercise after reading about it in *Awake and Aligned*. I was thoroughly enjoying the book, doing each exercise Nova recommends and having powerful experiences with them, when I came across her suggestion to make a list of activities that you enjoy and that bring you back into emotional alignment. I felt a strong resistance in me as I read that chapter, as if a voice were whispering in my head "No, we're not doing that. That's useless. We don't care about that. We've got important stuff to do." So, of course, since I didn't want to do the exercise, I knew that I had to do it, immediately.

I put her book down, took out my journal and started my list:
1_____

"Huh, that's funny," I thought. I couldn't really come up with anything that I enjoyed doing just for pure fun that wasn't also some part of my work, or my personal goal setting. I just sat there staring at the blank page for a few minutes, wondering what was wrong with me.

Until that moment, I had not realized that I wasn't having fun. I eventually came up with a few things, but the first big lesson I learned from this exercise is that I had lost touch with how to have fun, with what I actually liked to do for fun. Once I had a few things on my list, it became obvious to me that I hadn't done many of them in a long time.

So began the process of finding my Fun Self again. I worked on my list, including old activities and people and places I had forgotten about, and added in new things and experiences I had never had before. Most importantly, I began a deliberate process of going out and doing the things on my list and being conscious while doing them of how they made me feel.

I began hiking again, something I've loved all my life but had been neglecting lately. I went out alone and discovered new trails. My wife and I went out to our favorite trails and beaches. I bought some new books to read, invited a friend to play disc golf, and watched a movie with my son. I went to a local spa and soaked in a sensory deprivation tank and had a barbecue party for our friends and their families. I even began watching youtube tutorials on magic tricks and practiced them so I would have a few new moves to show the kids. In short, I was starting to have fun again.

In this manner I found my fun self, just as you will find your fun self, in two ways.

First, I was able to find my self, or experience my self, doing things I love much more often and on a much more consistent basis. Second, I was able to find my self, to be present and grateful, as each experience unfolded so that I could enjoy it even more.

Now you have the wonderful task of doing each and every thing on your Fun Self List. And discovering which items you really enjoy and want to repeat again and again, and which things are not a good fit anymore for you.

Make a powerful decision to do one thing on your list every day for seven days, or every week for seven weeks.

Then, after having such an amazing week, make a powerful decision to do one thing on your list every day for another 14 days, then another 21 days, and you will have 42 days straight of doing fun things off your list, of finding Your Fun Self, and you will have developed a completely new neural network, mapping you to Your Fun Self, and you will never lose that side of your self again.

Regardless of whether you take one action each day, or one each week, as you do the things on your list, embrace the activity and enjoy it as much as you can while it is happening. Then, after it is over, you can review the experience in your mind and judge how much you want to do it in the future, if at all.

In addition, look at your list and see if you can combine activities. If you like playing chess and being with people, but don't have many friends, can you start a game at a local coffee shop or join one at a local gaming store? If you like reading books and being outdoors, why not combine them and find a place at the beach, in the forest, or at the park to read? Be careful with this suggestion though. I can tell you from experience that some things just don't go well together, like my love of singing show tunes in the shower and my love of skydiving.

It's okay for some of the things on your list to have a practical purpose also. While you will want to make sure you include the frivolous fun, and the really relaxing or self pampering things, you can also include things that you enjoy that serve other purposes. For example, it is one of my personal goals, and something I take quite seriously, to run and lift weights on a consistent schedule each week, and to teach Tae Kwon Do classes each evening. And, I really enjoy it when I'm running: I've got my favorite inspirational music playing, my endorphins and dopamine are kicking in, the river I run by is beautiful, and I really like it. Running makes me happy. And the same is true when I'm in the gym, pumping the iron, or when I'm on the mat, teaching or training. I love that stuff!

One benefit of having added them to my Fun Self List is that I now see them not as chores, or tasks that I Have to accomplish, but as things I really enjoy and Get to do.

In a similar manner, I really enjoy gaining professional development in my field and I love to travel. I love going to seminars to learn new things, and once I recognize that this is something I truly enjoy and love doing, then it makes even more sense to invest in my own professional development and visit new places more often. In this way professional development and personal fulfillment become synonymous and a vacation expense for fun becomes a business investment for growth.

So have some fun with the process and take action today to find Your Fun Self.

Finding Your Fun Self
ACTIONS TO TAKE

1. Make a list of things that you enjoy doing, things that are fun, or relaxing, or exciting for you, that make you feel good.

My Fun List includes:

_____

_____

_____

_____

_____

_____

_____

_____

_____

_____

_____

_____

_____

_____

_____

2. Make a commitment to perform one item each day or week on your list, or select some upcoming dates by which you will do them.

Fun thing to do:

_____

_____

Date when I will do it:

_____

Fun thing to do:

_____

_____

Date when I will do it:

_____

Fun thing to do:

_____

_____

Date when I will do it:

_____

Fun thing to do:

_____

_____

Date when I will do it:

_____

_____

3. Be fully present and enjoy each experience in the moment, and after it's over decide whether to keep it on your list or not.

04 | FIND YOUR NATURAL SELF

As a child and teen I intuitively knew what scientific studies are now telling us: nature nurtures our self and our soul. From age 11 on, I would often take solo, survival camping trips, with just my bow, knife and matches, and make my own shelters and hunt and fish for food. Like many boys of that age, I was enamored of Indians and mountain men and keenly interested in wilderness survival.

On one trip I shot a cottontail earlier in the day with my bow and built a lean-to of thatched grass to sleep in for the night. I can still recall sitting in front of the lean-to roasting small bits of rabbit meat on green willow twigs and watching the flickering firelight dance with the deepening darkness. With a full belly, a warm fire, and a freshly-cut pile of big-bluestem to lie on, I was feeling quite contented and proud of myself. Although alone and surrounded by darkness, I felt completely at peace, secure and happy inside the circle of light cast by my small fire.

All of this was destroyed quite suddenly, however, when a long, drawn out wail erupted in the dark shadows of the night. I recognized it immediately as a coyote, one that was very close to my camp. Then, that first call was answered and soon several other canine voices joined the chorus, each emanating from a different direction.

The first few wails got my blood pumping, but once I realized that the coyotes had completely encircled my camp, I was positively panicked. I could hear them plainly now, calling to each other as they came closer and closer. Like it or not, the coyotes were closing in.

Of course, I knew that coyotes weren't really dangerous and didn't attack people, but such rational thoughts don't carry much weight when you're a child and you're alone in the wilderness at night. I could imagine the savory scent of the rabbit I had been roasting all evening wafting out on the cool night breeze, spreading itself across the land and calling the hungry coyotes in. I had also seen enough old movies and bad television to have plenty of unrealistic but completely horrifying images running through my mind of people being devoured by packs of wolves and wild dogs. My first thought was of defense. I quickly pulled the rabbit off the fire and threw on dried grass and kindling until the flames were leaping five foot high and projecting a fierce golden glow out into the night. Then, I grabbed my bow, nocked an arrow, loosened my knife in its sheath and put my back to the fire to face the night.

I strode around the small circle of light, walking its perimeter like a guard deep in enemy territory. For quite some time as I stood guard and trembled, they kept up their intermittent chorus, but the voices never came any closer. They remained somewhere out there in the darkness, keeping a respectful distance while they sang up the night.

After my fear subsided and it was clear that they weren't coming to attack me, I sat back down by the fire to relax and listen. I lay down on my soft bed of cut grass while the fire burned down to a bed of softly glowing orange coals and let the chorus of canine voices

FIELD NOTES

Spending time in nature has many benefits, especially in today's fast-paced, plugged in and turned-on world.

No matter where you live, you can find some natural areas to visit and enjoy.

wash over me. Many people are familiar with the call of a coyote, or have heard the lone howl of the wolf, but few have ever listened to an entire pack sing and celebrate in the night. High pitched yips punctuate the stillness of the night and melt into a long tremulous howl that is followed by others. Their voices rise and fall, tumbling over each other like playful cubs wrestling outside their mother's den. Each howl erupts from the chest and spreads itself over the landscape with its own personality. Some songs sound plaintive and haunting, others full of spirit and joy, while all melt into a single melody. The wild voices tug at something buried deep inside you, awakening your evolutionary origins, reminding you of your kinship with all life.

As my fire died down, the wild voices pulled me up off my grassy bower, and out into the night. I crept slowly and quietly away from the small clump of cottonwood and willow where my camp was set. Crouching in clumps of tall grass and running hunched over on all fours across the open areas, I probably could have been mistaken for a coyote, just one more member of the vociferous pack. As I listened to their song, my chest and throat felt like they were swelling with emotion, exploding with an energy that required some form of release. The first howl slipped from my throat almost of its own accord: a few tentative yips then a long lonely wail. It was answered from the side of a nearby hill, and then again by another voice coming from the ridge off to my right. I tried mimicking their voices, emulating the high pitched yips, and the tremulous rising and falling rhythm of the longer howls. They answered, speaking to each other and, it seemed, calling back to me. Sitting upright with the prairie-earth under my knees and the stalks of big bluestem rising over my head, I imagined myself a coyote, encircled by an earthen embrace. I looked out across the tumbling landscape of flint hills, rolling prairie and shadowed woodland, and together, we sang up the land and prayed to the night. A pack of wild brethren, coyotes one and all.

Spending time in nature has many benefits, especially in today's fast-paced, plugged-in and turned-on world. It is good for us to take some time to detach from the noise and distractions, and enjoy the peace of the natural world. There is nothing quite like looking up at the milky way, and the vast expanse of stars and inky blackness to give perspective, nothing quite like the soothing sounds of the wind whispering in the trees or the ocean waves rhythmically crashing on the beach to calm the soul.

Some of the most obvious benefits of getting outdoors are the emotional and physical benefits of getting exercise and fresh air. Natural areas where plants are growing are high in oxygen, and we take bigger breaths when we exercise, and produce a host of feel-good neuro-chemicals from dopamine to endorphins. Add to this the added vitamin D from sunlight, metabolic and cardio-vascular benefits of regular exercise, and "getting outdoors" becomes a recipe for complete physical and emotional health.

In addition, natural places with moving water, such as beaches, lakeshores, and riverbanks, are high in negative ions. When we absorb these negative ions they have a positive emotional benefit and lift our mood. Many physicians have begun prescribing time in nature to patients suffering from Seasonal Affective Disorder and in Japan the practice of Shinrin-Yoku, or forest bathing, has been used for decades to promote physical and psychological health.

Finally, whether you are walking in a forest, hiking up a mountain, sitting on a park bench, or lying down on the beach, you are giving your self the time and space to be alone, to let the incessant chattering of the monkey mind quiet down, and to reflect on who you are, what you value, and what you want.

No matter where you live, you can find some natural areas to visit and enjoy. You might be lucky enough to live near a beach, lake, river, or wetland that you can visit. Or you may have hiking trails in the mountains or forests near your home. Or, perhaps there are city parks, arboretums or gardens you can visit.

You might discover hiking or biking trails that you can explore, or you may find a nice spot where you can simply sit and enjoy the sounds and sights of nature. You might decide to go on extended backpacking trips in the wilderness, or brief visits to your local park, university campus, or abandoned field.

Regardless of where you live and what opportunities to commune with nature you are already aware of, do some research and discover new places to go locally where you have never been before. Look up local trails, parks and nature areas and visit your local bookstore to find local hiking and outing guides.

You might decide to make a game out of it and collect pictures of sunsets from different places, or take a field guide and identify native plants and animals. You might decide to link finding your Natural Self with your other goals, like a fitness goal and go trail running, or a painting or drawing goal and sit and draw. You might decide to take a partner with you, or to share your newly found favorite spots with others, or to go there alone.

Regardless of how you choose to engage with nature, here are a few suggestions for using your experiences in the natural world to Find Your Natural Self.

First, make one, or several, of your trips into a vision quest. That means going alone, or having a partner who is also using the journey in the same way and doing the same things as you. So if you're comfortable backpacking or camping, then make it a solo camp, and do it alone. Or, if you are a hiker or beachcomber, take a few trips by your self and enjoy the solitude. Or, if you must bring a partner for safety or security reasons, have them read this chapter, and commit to their own vision quest with you.

If you are a very active person, make sure that you spend some time sitting quietly in nature, watching, thinking and doing nothing. Bring your journal with you and give your self several different opportunities to write about: Who you are? What you value? What makes you happy? What gives you meaning? And so on.

Practice the Harmonize with Nature Meditation. For this meditation find a comfortable place in your chosen natural area to sit down. Find some aspect of the natural landscape that is moving and focus your attention on it. Perhaps you can see the rhythmic swaying of trees blowing in the breeze, or the waves crashing on the beach, or a stream flowing by. Soften your gaze and use the

Head to Toe Relax and the Ten to One Countdown (described in Chapter 5: Finding Your Spiritual Self) to relax your self down into a meditative state.

As you soften your gaze and focus on the movement of nature in front of you, allow your self to begin to feel the same rhythm of moving energy inside you. You might even sway a little back and forth where you sit. Let that energy and the rhythm of its movement harmonize with your breathing, your heart beating, the thoughts flitting in and out of your mind. Enjoy this peaceful state for as long as you want, then journal about your meditative experience afterward.

After you have gone on your vision quest and discovered some places in nature that you love to go, share the experience with someone you enjoy. Invite a friend or family member to join you and share your favorite spots with them.

Finally, you will enjoy your experiences much more, and be more prepared to handle your self, if you make it a practice to learn about the native plants and wildlife in the places you visit. Buy a field guide to local plants, birds and other wildlife and make a habit of learning about them on each trip. When you increase your ecological literacy in this way, going for a walk in the woods is like walking in your neighborhood and seeing friends all over the place: "oh hello redwood, and trillium flower," you say, and "hi there blackberry and salmon berry, and hello again solomon's seal and yarrow."

Ecological literacy is a term that refers to being able to read the landscape you are in like a book, to know the native flora and fauna, weather patterns, local history and so on. One way of finding your self is to find out more about where you are in physical space. So, learning more about your place in the world is one way to learn more about your self.

In time (and space) you will find your self much more connected to your place in the world and then you will have found Your Natural Self.

Finding Your Natural Self
ACTIONS TO TAKE

1. Visit some natural spots on a regular basis, by your self, and bring your journal as you make your trip into a vision quest. As you work on your list below, do some research if necessary (buy a local trail guidebook or explore online to find places to visit).

Natural Places I can visit:

_____

_____

_____

_____

_____

_____

_____

_____

_____

_____

_____

_____

_____

_____

_____

_____

_____

_____

_____

_____

_____

_____

_____

_____

_____

2. Spend some time journaling and reflecting while you are there and record your thoughts and insights in your journal. Record your insights from your first new journey here:

Reflections during my first natural journey:

_____

_____

_____

_____

_____

_____

_____

_____

_____

_____

_____

3. Practice the harmonize with nature meditation while you are on your natural journey and record your experiences and insights in your journal. Record your insights from your first harmonize with nature meditation here.

Insights from my first harmonize with nature journey:

_____

_____

_____

_____

_____

_____

_____

_____

_____

_____

_____

_____

_____

_____

_____

_____

_____

_____

_____

05 | FIND YOUR SPIRITUAL SELF

Fear has many consequences. One of the first and most powerful consequences of fear is that it makes us hurry. Fear makes us rush to fix things. And in that rushing, we make mistakes, and things get worse.

One summer I was working for the Forest Service monitoring water quality in streams high up in the Sierras. My partner and I had been working a remote area all day and had a plan to rendezvous with the rest of our group at a camping spot we all knew well, right beside a mountain lake. That morning we took only our survey equipment and daypacks with food, water and jackets with us. The rest of our gear, tents, sleeping bags, stoves, and so on, we left with the team that was tasked with moving camp.

Unfortunately for us that meant we were about to get very cold and wet. One of those powerful summer storms that are surprisingly common at high elevations came down upon the mountains with a vengeance. First it dumped rain, soaking everything and the wind howled in icy gusts. We put on every piece of clothing we had and still we were soaked and frozen to the bone. Then the rain turned to hail, pelting us with hard hail stones and dropping the temperature even further, and then it turned back to rain again.

By the time we reached the assigned camping place, both of our lips were blue. We were on the edge of hypothermia and no one else was there to meet us. The campsite was empty. No warm clothes. No tents. No fire. Nothing.

They should have been there hours before us and we were beginning to get scared about what we would do if they never showed up with our gear. Our first instinct was to find them, to find our gear. We thought about going back to the old base camp, or looking for them on the trail that led from that camp to this lake. We wondered if they had gotten lost or were looking for us.

If we had given in to that fear, we would have gone desperately looking for them and our dry gear. If we had panicked, we would have started running down the trail toward the old base camp, through the storm, on slick ground, getting colder and risking injury every step of the way. Instead, shivering and soaked to the bone, and still getting drenched by rain and whipped about by the freezing wind, we sat down, stayed calm and took a few moments to assess our situation. We decided the only important thing was to get dry and warm and stay put until our friends and gear arrived, or the storm passed.

Within thirty minutes of looking, we found a cave-like overhang that would keep us out of the wind and rain. There was even a huge pile of dry pine needles and wood in the back of the cave, so soon we had a fire roaring and steam coming off of our drying clothes.
When the rest of the team finally made it to the lake with all the gear, they found us sitting contentedly by a campfire, in a dry cave, sipping hot tea and eating trail mix.

Of course, the worst thing you can do when you are lost in the wilderness is to panic. Even if you don't injure your self and become even more lost from running around like a crazy person, the fear and panic still erode your ability to function. When we are scared and stressed our brain wave levels begin to speed up, from lower to higher levels of Beta, and we actually use less of our brain. In addition our neurological system floods the brain with neuro-inhibitors which slow the synaptic connections. So, fear, panic and stress actually make us dumber.

On the other hand, MRI's show that when we relax ourselves into a meditative state, our brain waves slow down from Beta to Alpha, and much more of our brain lights up, or is accessed and used. In addition, as we relax, we produce neuro-transmitters which increase and improve synaptic connections. So, when we relax and meditate we actually become smarter.

Therefore, whether you are lost in a mountain wilderness or in the wilderness of your life, the advice I'm going to give you is the same:

"Don't just do something, sit there."

 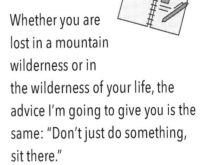
If you're lost in the woods, sit down, calm down and take some time to assess the situation. Then you will be able to make a much better decision about what action to take.

Similarly, if you have been getting lost in the daily wilderness of life, taking some time each day to quietly slow down, will help you know which direction to go.

Engaging in a regular practice of meditation will help you to quiet your mind and all the noise and stress from your daily life, so that you can access that Inner Self, Your Spiritual Self.

You don't need to contort your self into difficult positions or join a monastery in order to meditate well and successfully. Simply find a place where you can sit comfortably without being disturbed for 10-30 minutes, close your eyes, and allow your self to relax.

In order to relax your self down into a meditative state use one or both of the following practices: First, The Head to Toe Relax and Second the Ten to One countdown. If you have not meditated much before, I recommend doing both relaxation techniques before every meditation session. After a few months of meditation, you may find that you only need to use one of the relaxation techniques, or only need to countdown from 3 to 1, in order to achieve your desired, meditative state.

The Head to Toe Relax
Sit in a comfortable position, take a few deep and relaxed breaths and close your eyes. Speak to your self silently in your mind in a very relaxed and soothing voice. Start at the top of your head and work down your body slowly, saying things like "I can feel a raindrop of relaxation land on top of my head and wash slowly over my entire body. I can feel the muscles of my scalp and face loosening and relaxing. I can feel the warm and relaxing feelings wash down my neck and shoulders loosening and relaxing the muscles of my back..."

Continue in this same manner until you have relaxed your self all the way from the top of your head to the tips of your fingers and toes.

The 10 to 1 Countdown
After completing the head to toe relax, tell your self in that same soothing voice that you are going to count down from ten to one. Tell your self that each time you say a number you will see it in your mind and you will feel your relaxation double and deepen. Then begin slowly counting down by saying, for example "10. I can feel my relaxation double and deepen. 9. I am even more relaxed. 8. And again I can feel myself relaxing further and deeper still..."
Once you have relaxed your self down into Alpha brain wave levels, you can engage in any form of meditation that you wish. I will suggest three here. You might choose to use one form of meditation on one day, and a different method on the following day. Or you might choose to combine two or three of these methods and do all of them in a single session. Experiment and do what works best for you.

Still Mind Meditation

The Still Mind Meditation is one of the most commonly taught and unfortunately one of the most difficult forms of meditation. The goal is to quiet the monkey mind, to turn off that incessant internal dialogue and chatter. The difficulty many beginners find, however, is that it can be very hard to empty the mind and not think. The simplest thing to do is to focus on your breathing, to notice each breath coming in and each breath going out. Focus on the feel of the air going through your nostrils, the rise and fall of your stomach and chest, and so on. As thoughts arise in your mind (which they will) such as "what should I cook for dinner tonight? I've got to pick the kids up this afternoon. I can't believe he talked to me like that. Am I doing this right?" just notice them, name them as a thought and let them go. Then return your attention to your breathing.

And when the next thought arises, notice it, and let it go, and return your attention to your breathing. In and Out. In and Out. In and Out.

Visual Motor Rehearsal

Visual Motor Rehearsal is used in sports to help athletes improve their performance, and it can be used to improve anything we do. Research has shown that when athletes visualize themselves performing, the neurons in their body fire in the exact same order as when they physically practice. By repeatedly visualizing themselves successfully competing, they can significantly improve their performance.

In this use of Visual Motor Rehearsal you will choose one or several things you want to enjoy doing or improve your performance in. Then, just like watching a movie, or daydreaming with your eyes closed, see and hear your self performing flawlessly and enjoying the experience immensely.

You might choose to watch your self succeed at an upcoming job interview or speech, or to see your self jogging and exercising each day, or drinking tea at night instead of alcohol, or spending time with someone you love. As you enjoy watching your self succeed, spin those feelings of confidence and joy and pride faster and bigger and really feel the feeling of success inside you.

Connecting with Your Higher Power
Every religion teaches that when we enter a meditative, prayerful or reflective state we can gain greater access to, or connection with, our higher power, spirit guides, guardian angels, universal energy, collective consciousness, or God. (Choose whichever word you prefer).

For this meditation make a clear intention that you will connect with your higher power or spirit guides. Feel your self floating up out of your body and look back to see your body sitting below you. You may notice a thin, silvery thread connecting your spirit to your body, which will always bring you back to your body when you are done with your journey. Feel your self float up into the sky and imagine a place where you can meet your angels or guides. Perhaps this will be a castle, or temple, or maybe a cave or a meadow in the woods, whatever works best for you.

Call in and ask for your God, or Guides, or Angels to be present and give you their aid. Imagine them joining you and spend some time with them. You might talk to them, or look at them, or feel your self vibrating with their same frequency. In whatever way feels fitting to you, spend some time with these spirit guides and feel their power and wisdom entering you and filling you up. Then return to your meditating body.

Whatever form of meditation works best for you, engage in it as often as possible. You will find that not only is there a wilderness outdoors to explore, there is also one within. Explore your inner wilderness and find your Spiritual Self now.

You can also develop, explore and express your Spiritual Self through communion with others and independent study.

Depending upon your own spiritual interest and understanding, you can develop it further through studying that faith or philosophy more diligently. Find out what books you could read to learn more about your spiritual beliefs and practice. There may be specific teachers, authors, or masters in your spiritual tradition who you can learn more about and whose work you can follow. Perhaps you will learn more about the history of your spiritual tradition, or how to practice it in daily life.

Or, maybe you don't know what your spiritual tradition is. In that case, I recommend reading the main sacred texts of some of the most major religions: The Bible, both Old and New Testament, the Koran, Buddhist Sutras, Black Elk Speaks, the Bhagavad Gita, the Tripitaka, the Tao Te Ching, and so on. Or another place to start in deepening your Spiritual Self is by reading contemporary writers and studying with any of the many spiritually oriented teachers working today, whether that is in person, via online classes or simply listening to podcasts or other media. There are many ways you can learn more about and enjoy connecting to whatever spiritual tradition is right for you.

As we develop and explore our Spiritual Self, and the borders of our faith and practice, it helps to find others. Discover what seminars or lectures you could attend and which organizations or fellowships you might join? What teachers might you want to meet or what holy places would you like to visit? Perhaps there is a church, mosque, synagogue, fellowship, meditation group, witches circle, or philosophical organization that you might join.

Make a list at the end of this chapter of resources you could use to experience and express your Spiritual Self and add to this list as you do research on the subject. Then go out and get some of these resources and immerse your self in the study of your Spiritual Self, as you also find others to share and express your Spiritual Self with, and you will discover that you have been found and saved!

Finding Your Spiritual Self
ACTIONS TO TAKE

1. Keep up a daily, or almost daily, meditation practice, of at least 10-20 minutes, for 40 days. Use the head to toe relax and the 10-1 countdown to start your mediation. Make note of any important insights, new awareness, or ideas you have, while meditating and throughout the rest of your day. Record your insights and experiences for the first week here.

Day 1: Type of Meditation Performed:

_____

_____

Insights or experiences:

_____

_____

_____

_____

_____

_____

_____

_____

_____

_____

_____

Day 2: Type of Meditation Performed:

_____

_____

Insights or experiences:

_____

_____

_____

_____

_____

_____

_____

Day 3: Type of Meditation Performed:

_____

_____

Insights or experiences:

_____

_____

_____

_____

_____

_____

_____

Day 4: Type of Meditation Performed:

_____

_____

Insights or experiences:

_____

_____

_____

_____

_____

_____

_____

Day 5: Type of Meditation Performed:

_____

_____

Insights or experiences:

_____

_____

_____

_____

_____

_____

_____

Day 6: Type of Meditation Performed:

_____

_____

Insights or experiences:

_____

_____

_____

_____

_____

_____

_____

Day 7: Type of Meditation Performed:

_____

_____

Insights or experiences:

_____

_____

_____

_____

_____

_____

_____

2. Make a list of resources you can use to find your Spiritual Self: Books, authors, teachers, seminars, and spiritual groups and organizations.

_____

_____

_____

_____

_____

_____

_____

_____

_____

_____

_____

_____

_____

_____

_____

_____

_____

_____

_____

_____

(to be continued by you in your journal)

06 | FIND YOUR PHYSICAL SELF

To start with, let's find out where you are in physical space.

Let your eyes wander off the sides of the page to the fingers and hands holding this book. Then let your gaze and awareness rise up the arms to your shoulders. Now, let your awareness settle into the space just above and below your neck, into your head and your heart, and now bring that awareness to your entire body.

Congratulations, you just found your self. This is you, physically.

Where you are, is called "Here." And you are always Here.

And When you are, is called "Now"." And you are always Now.

So, You are Here and You are Now.

No matter what you do, no matter how many different places you go to, or adventures you go on, you will always know exactly where and when you are. Here and Now.

So, remember where you are and let's go find your self.

One of the most common mistakes people make once they realize they are lost in the wilderness is that they panic and get in a hurry. They get in a rush to find the path or a landmark they recognize and they begin running around, not being careful, so concerned about getting found that they forget to take care of themselves. Then, they stumble and sprain an ankle or twist a knee, or they fall and break an arm or get a concussion. Or they run around in the afternoon sun and get heat stroke, or in a rainstorm and get hypothermia. Now, in addition to being lost, they have it even worse: they are injured or ill.

Once their health or physical body is compromised they don't have the ability to save themselves anymore. They lack the fitness or energy, they are in too much pain, and they simply can't handle the physical challenges required to get found. So, unless someone else rescues them, they end up dying alone in the wilderness.

I was training a team of Conservation Corps members in Death Valley one summer on desert survival scenarios when we were called to help look for a missing hiker. The man had been dropped off in the morning at one end of a trail by his wife, for a several hour hike. The plan was for his wife to pick him up around noon at the other end of the trail, except he never showed up. After waiting a couple of hours, his wife alerted park rangers that he was late and the search began.

When he was found that evening, he was several miles from the trail, completely out of water and dead from heat stroke and dehydration. Apparently he had gotten off the trail and realized he was lost. At this point, if he was thinking clearly, he could have hunkered down in the shade and rested through the hottest part of the day while awaiting rescue. He would probably have been embarrassed but he would have been alive when he was found.

Instead, fear and panic must have set in once he realized he was lost in the desert and he began hiking fast and hard trying desperately to find the trail again. I imagine he also didn't want to suffer the embarrassment of having to be rescued and was so desperate to find the way himself that he neglected his own physical health.

In the searing heat and blazing afternoon sun, he continued to hike hard, scrambling up rocky ridges and down gullies, until finally he was so fatigued with heat stroke and dehydration he could hike no more and it was all over.

Now, we know that you don't want to die in the desert and that this is not your fate. So, let's take some time to pay attention to, and take care of, that body of yours, to help you find your next, best Physical Self.

What do you need to do to enjoy and embrace your physical body more?

The answers you come up with don't have to be only about gaining better health or fitness, either. Start a list of all the different things you can do that will get you in touch with your body, things that will help you enjoy and experience it.

Of course, your list might start with eating a healthier diet and getting better nutrition. It might include eating more salads, vegetables and fish instead of red meat and carbs. It might include taking a good regimen of daily vitamins, drinking more water, or losing weight.

You might want to get in better shape physically and improve your health and fitness by walking or jogging, swimming, doing yoga or martial arts, lifting weights, or joining a health club. You might want to experience your self as someone who can run a marathon or triathlon, or as someone who has lost or gained 30 pounds.

You might want to experience your self as someone who gives up smoking, or alcohol or drinking coffee or sodas.

In addition to experiencing your self as someone who takes better care of their body, you should get to experience your self as someone who enjoys their body more. So, add to your list all the ways you can think of to enjoy, pamper, and appreciate Your Physical Self more.

Maybe it's time for a haircut and some new styles of clothes to update your image and how you feel about how you look. Maybe it's time to indulge your self in that spa treatment or in getting a massage on a regular basis. Or maybe you would like to sleep better at night, so you need to get some new sheets and pillows and do some research on herbal teas and natural sleep remedies.

What are those fun things, those things that give you pleasure, that you like to do with your body? Dancing, swimming, having sex, sunbathing, sleeping, etc.? Add those to your list.

And ask your self for each thing on your list, how can I enjoy more of that activity and how can I enjoy that activity more?

Once you have come up with some items on your list for finding your best Physical Self, decide on the steps you can take to get started.

If better fitness and nutrition are goals of yours, then do some research on the best nutritional diets for your purposes and body type, and start an exercise and eating journal where you record all of your snacks, meals and workouts. Find a workout partner or class to join to hold you accountable and support you in your efforts and take powerful action.

If going hiking, or dancing, or getting a massage is on your list for ways you would like to enjoy your body, then look up your local trails, what bands are playing and what dance classes there are, and schedule that next massage or spa appointment today.

Whatever it is that's on your list of ways to enjoy, experience and appreciate your body more, make sure that you do it. Because you only get one body in this life time. This one is it. That's all you get, so make sure to take good care of it.

Think about it this way: For most of us, when we were kids it was someone else's responsibility to feed and take care of our bodies (probably our parents or grandparents). At some point, though, when we moved out of the home and became adults, that responsibility became ours.

Now imagine that on the day you turned 18 and moved out of the house I came to you and said "I'm giving you a car for your very own. I've been doing all the upkeep and maintenance on it until now, but from now on, it's your car and you have to be responsible to take care of it. And, you don't have to pay me. You are getting the car for free. There's just one catch: It's the only car you will ever get for the rest of your life."

How carefully do you think you would treat that car? Would you be doing burn outs, driving crazy, running it on bad gas, neglecting to get the oil changed and do other maintenance? Or, would you treat that car with care: follow all the recommended maintenance suggestions, wash and clean it regularly, and take care not to wreck it or ruin it, and give it the best fuel possible?

Well, this is precisely the position you are in right now and for the rest of your life. You only have one vehicle to get you where you are going—Your Physical Self—so you better take good care of it and enjoy and appreciate it.

It's also important to realize that it is never too late to start. I remember one student who powerfully taught me this lesson at Sun Yi's Academy in Topeka, Kansas, GrandMaster Yi's School. She was testing for her 3rd Dan Black Belt and it was her 70th birthday. She had brought a picture of herself from the day she started Tae Kwon Do and there she was, standing with her white belt on, ten years younger than today. And yet, in the picture, she looked ten years older than the woman standing before us wearing the black belt. After ten years of training Tae Kwon Do, she had not aged ten years, she had become ten years younger!

That's the power of taking care of your Body Temple. You don't have to be in great shape to start taking care of your self, but you have to start taking care of your self to get in great shape.

So, when would Now be a good time to start?

Finding Your Physical Self
ACTIONS TO TAKE

1. Make a list of things you can do, or stop doing, or do better, in order to improve your physical health and take those actions: (ranging from better nutrition, exercise, hydration and sleep, to stopping drinking or smoking)

Things I can DO to improve my health:

_____

_____

_____

_____

_____

_____

_____

_____

_____

_____

_____

_____

_____

_____

_____

_____

Things I can STOP doing to improve my health:

_____

_____

_____

_____

_____

_____

_____

_____

_____

_____

_____

_____

_____

_____

_____

2. Make a list of things you can do to pamper your self physically that you should do more often (naps, spa treatments, eating at a restaurant, getting new clothes or a haircut, etc.)

Things I can ENJOY physically:

_____

_____

_____

_____

_____

_____

_____

_____

_____

_____

_____

_____

_____

_____

_____

_____

_____

3. In order to get started, choose a few things off your list above, and list out the steps you need to take in order to do it, or the date on which you are committed to doing it.

I will Stop doing:

_____

_____

_____

_____

_____

_____

Steps along the way and dates when I will take them:

_____

_____

_____

_____

_____

_____

_____

_____

_____

_____

I will Start Doing to Improve my Health:

_____

_____

_____

_____

_____

_____

_____

_____

_____

_____

_____

Steps along the way and dates when I will take them:

_____

_____

_____

_____

_____

_____

_____

_____

_____

_____

_____

_____

_____

_____

_____

I will Start Doing to Enjoy my Body:

_____

_____

_____

_____

_____

_____

Steps along the way and dates when I will take them:

_____

_____

_____

_____

_____

_____

_____

_____

_____

_____

_____

_____

_____

(to be continued by you in your journal)

07 | FIND YOUR NEW SELF

I was teaching a team land navigation, map and compass skills, in the thick redwood forests and rugged coastal mountains of northern California on a very wet, fall day when we learned a lesson about the value of doing something new.

I showed them how to find our location on the map, where we wanted to go, and how to take a compass bearing to that location that you could follow to get there. In between us and our destination lay a thick forest of 200 foot tall trees and a maze of streams and ridges, with no visible landmarks in site.

At first the team decided to follow the compass bearing directly toward our intended location, thinking that the shortest distance between two points is a straight line. However, the landscape seemed to keep putting obstacles in our way and pushing us to the left. A huge ridge would appear in front of us and to our right, forcing us to veer left. Then, when we tried to correct our course again, a vast thicket of blown down trees or some other obstacle would appear and push us left again.

After letting the team fight the landscape for a couple hours, desperately trying to stay on their original compass bearing I asked everyone to stop. We all were soaking wet and muddy from clambering up rain-soaked slopes and pushing through thick underbrush. They were tired and frustrated.

I asked them if they wanted to stick to the original compass bearing or if they could think of a different strategy to follow. After some discussion and consultation of the map, they realized that if we followed the landscape left, or downstream (the way the land wanted us to go) long enough, we would eventually end up at the bottom of the valley we were aiming for. Then, we could hike back upstream, to the right, up that valley to get back to our target location.

With two new compass bearings to follow, we took off and enjoyed pleasant streamside hiking the rest of the way and the landscape never seemed to get in our way again. We could have kept going however, insisting that we stay true to our original compass bearing. We could have stayed stuck in that rut, but instead, once it was clear that it wasn't working, we chose to do something new.

Sometimes in life you get lost because you get stuck in a rut.

You get caught in a pattern of thinking and feeling and doing the same things and you are
caught in a neurological loop that you are barely aware of and cannot control.

You are walking around in circles, lost in the wilderness, and getting even more lost as you go.

You need a shift. You need a new direction.

You need to be jolted out of your rut. You need to be pushed and pulled and shocked from your path.

60

Because, if you are reading this, it means you've gotten stuck and let your self stay lost.

You know you have.

You've been taking things for granted.

You've been slacking.

You've been shirking your duties and shrinking from life.

You've lost your enjoyment and appreciation for what you have.

That's why you are reading this: Because it's time to change, and change is here now, and you know it, and you are ready for it.

So, instead of walking around in circles, doing the same old things, it's time to do something new. It's time to do something different.

It is time to...

Do something new you have never done before.

Learn something new you have never learned before.

Go somewhere new you have never gone before.

Meet someone new you have never met before.

Really push your self to stretch your mind and think about what are some really new and different things you could do.

Maybe you could take flying lessons and learn how to fly an airplane or a hang-glider or go skydiving. Go ahead, look up your local airport and flight schools and take that first lesson.

I remember the day I took my first flying lesson. I was so excited as I drove to the airport that I felt like a kid on Christmas morning. In fact, I was so excited that I was actually nervous, maybe even slightly scared.

Everything we did was novel, important and exciting. Just sitting in the classroom and listening to the instructor and doing the pre-flight inspection of the airplane, had me buzzing with enthusiasm. And then, oh that moment, when I pushed the throttle forward and the plane took off and was flying under my own control: that was exquisite! After an hour of flying, when I brought that plane down onto the runway, landed, taxied to the side and came to a full stop, I couldn't stop smiling and that smile lasted for days.

It was such an amazing experience for me that I had to wonder why I had been thinking about it for years, wanting to do it, and yet had waited so long to begin.

What is it that you have been hesitating to do?

Maybe you could go to Las Vegas and see Cirque de So Le or to New York to catch a Broadway Show, or to Disney World with the family, or go to a play at your local theater.

Maybe you could climb a mountain or go on a meditation retreat, or take a cruise or go to Hawaii.

Maybe you could volunteer at the local food bank or shelter, join a choir, or take a class.

Maybe there is a skill you would like to develop like playing music, painting, carpentry, dancing, welding, cooking, designing websites, gardening, or doing massage.

Maybe there is something you would like to learn about like quantum physics, or local history, or computer programming, or philosophy, or creative writing.

Maybe there is somewhere you've never been that you would like to visit, historic sites or state or national parks, someplace close to home or maybe some country or culture far away.

While you are dreaming about and planning these big, new things, find small ways to "New" the ordinary, or do ordinary things in new ways. This helps break old neurological loops and habits, and helps to broaden the mind.

Drive a new route to work. Sleep on the other side of the bed. Cook a new meal. Write, eat, or text with your non-dominant hand. Sit on a different spot on the couch. Find new ways to do old things and have some fun with it.

There are two vital purposes in doing something completely new. First, it will break you out of your rut and keep you from walking around in circles looking like a lost idiot. And second, it answers the human need for growth.

All living beings need to grow. We are either living and growing or dead and decaying. There is no other choice. And in order to grow, we have to encounter, experience, and do new things, things we haven't done before.

When we are growing and learning we are happy and fulfilled.

Fortunately there has never been a better time to want to learn something new. We have more access to information, teachers, classes and places than ever before in history. There have never been more books than we have in print now; never have there been so many instructional videos, blogs and websites, so many online classes and teachers. And it has never been as easy to travel as it is now.

Now is the perfect time to begin learning and doing something new and you can begin that journey from the comfort of your own home and then see where it takes you.

Once you come up with one or several ideas begin brainstorming and researching the different ways you can get started.

You could buy a book or watch an instructional video on youtube. You could find a useful blog or website online, or a webinar or class to join. You could research the history of somewhere you want to visit and the best attractions to see when you are there. You could find a local group, organization, or class in your area to join, or a tutor who can teach you.

Take that first step and then let it lead you to others, until you are walking the path.

Maybe your epic hike along the Andean trail to Machu Picchu will begin with the first step of renewing your passport and buying a book on the ancient Incas. Then, you might find your self researching the options and prices for guides and packaged tours. A few more steps and you find your self hiking regularly on local trails near your home while wearing your new hiking boots and backpack to get in shape for the journey. A few more steps and you are saving money for the trip, reading articles and blogs on tourist websites, and beginning to pick out travel dates. Then you're on the airplane and then traveling by rickety bus through the rugged mountains, and then, finally, you step out onto the trail, camp under the stars, and find your self exploring the massive ruins.

And it all began with that very first step, with that decision to do something new.

Now it is your time to decide. Your New Self is waiting to be found. So make a powerful decision today to Do something New, and to New whatever you Do!

Finding Your New Self
ACTIONS TO TAKE

1. Make a list of things you have never done before, places you have never visited, and subjects about which you might like to learn.

New Things, Places, and Subjects I can Explore:

_____

_____

_____

_____

_____

_____

_____

_____

_____

_____

_____

_____

_____

_____

_____

_____

2. Take New Action: Buy a book or enroll in a course to learn that new subject or skill, and take a trip to visit that new place, or to do that thing you have never done.

Actions I can take on one New thing from above:

_____

_____

_____

_____

_____

Actions I can take on a Second New thing from above:

_____

_____

_____

_____

_____

Actions I can take on a third New thing from above:

_____

_____

_____

_____

_____

(continue with other New things from your list above)

3. Notice which new things you enjoy and continue to pursue them and remember to "New what you Do" at the same time that you "Do the New!"

08 | FIND YOUR BETTER SELF

There are lots of ways of being lost, and lots of moments of finding your self again.

There are moments of complete desperation, of knowing you have no idea where you are, and then there are moments of slight confusion, and questions of direction and distance. Each one represents a different degree of being lost.

Sometimes people get completely lost. They lose all track of the trail, the direction home. They starve in the wilderness, join gangs or political parties, develop addictions or mental and physical illnesses, or relationship or financial problems which only serve to distract them from who they truly are.

At other times, people get just turned around a little bit. They are just momentarily unsure of the way home. They get a little lost, for a while, in parenting and careers, in success and their reputation, all of which only serves to distract them from who they truly are.

There are many ways of getting lost and many ways of getting found.

When you are exploring in the wilderness without trails there are many moments where you lose your self. You are not exactly sure where you are. You have a basic idea, you hope, but you're not completely sure and there is no way to be completely sure. It could be this drainage or that one? It could be 5 more miles or 7?

But you don't show this lack of certainty to your group. Because, basically, you do know where you are: You know that if you keep going on this heading, eventually, you'll hit the road you're aiming for. It might be after climbing one ridge or two or three. It might mean turning right or left once you hit the road and hiking another mile or two. But, none of that matters.

Because you have to face your fear. You have to face that uncertainty head on. You have to admit your fear inside: "I'm afraid because I don't know exactly where I am, but I don't want to show it." "Because, I know where we are. I know where I am at and what direction I'm headed. Kind of...."

That partial knowledge and the ability to adapt as you go, means you don't have to be 100% sure. You only have to know which is the most promising direction for now. You don't need to know the details of the route. Those you will discover along the way.

It's like driving across country at night. You don't have to see all the hundreds of miles in front of you that you have to travel. All you have to see is the 200 feet in front of you, illuminated by your headlights and you can drive on and on, through the darkness, for countless miles and years, while your path is revealed before you.

So, what is it that you are uncertain of?

Whether you are completely lost or just a little turned around in your life doesn't matter. In both cases you know what your fear is. You know what the problem is and you're afraid to admit it.

You may not know how to go about it, but you have to face that fear head on and you can trust that the way will be shown to you as you walk it.

So, what is it that you are afraid of? Where are you scared that you're getting lost?

Are you afraid you're getting lost in your job or relationship, in financial problems or addictions?

Where is your weak spot?

About what are you afraid?

What is that one thing you should quit?

What is that one thing you should start?

FIELD NOTES

Write it down:

Your greatest fear or obstacle. The one thing you most need to change.

Now, what would happen if you did that?

We have all been there before. We know there is something we need to stop or start doing and we know we will be better for it once we make that change. However, the change scares us. We don't want to give up the familiar and the comfortable. In fact, we will often suffer the familiar consequences of inaction for years, even though they are torturing us, because we are more afraid of the change.

The certainty of suffering seems less daunting than the uncertainty of change. This is why people stay in jobs they hate, fail to leave abusive relationships and struggle to give up addictions.

Think about it this way. You know that if you don't make a change you will continue to suffer and you know that you are afraid to make that change. So, you resign your self to avoid making the change, or you put it off in your mind, saying you will do it next month or next year. What this really means is that you are planning to suffer. You are planning to keep doing the thing that makes you suffer and to avoid the change that will make you feel better. You are planning to continue hurting your self.

Honestly, that sounds like shitty plan to me.

How about we come up with a different plan, a better plan, a plan to find Your Better Self, a plan to go in a better direction? How about we come up with a plan to name your biggest fear and then to confront it directly and get rid of it forever? How does that sound for a plan?

Write it down: Your greatest fear or obstacle. The one thing you most need to change.

I'll wait. I'm patient.

Go ahead and skip to the back of the chapter and write that one thing down.

Now, what would happen if you did that?

Imagine you already are that Better Self and write about it. Write a story where you describe each step and detail of you taking that action and it working out better than you could have imagined. Go ahead and write it down. I'll wait. I'm very patient. Skip the end of the chapter and start writing your success story of becoming your better self.

When I was a small child, our neighbor had this giant sheep dog, which was notorious around the neighborhood for jumping up on picnic tables and ruining picnics, knocking kids off their bikes and bowling old ladies over. If he was outside when I left the house to go to my tree fort in the back yard he would chase me like the devil he was. It was always a combination between making geometric calculations on the fly—would his line and rate of travel intersect my line and rate of travel before the ladder or after?—and succeeding at the fastest adrenaline-soaked, heart-pounding 100 yard dash you can imagine.

One day it was clear to me that I was not going to make it to the ladder in time to escape his snapping jaws and sharp canines. I had dozens of yards to go and I could feel his hot breath on my ankles as I ran. Just when I felt like he was on top of me, I spun around suddenly and grabbed the long hair on top of his head and held on firmly. He tried to wrestle away for a minute, but couldn't turn his head to bite my arm or escape from the vise-like grip my fear-fueled fingers had on his hair.

Then, he just sat down, wagged his tail and began panting in a calm and resigned way. From that day forward he never chased me again and I was never afraid of him.

Once we face them, most of our fears turn out to be paper tigers, just like that dog. They might look scary from far away, but once we get close and face them directly, we see that they are all illusion, all smoke and no fire.

Now it is time for you to face your fear and overcome it. Now it is time to turn that obstacle into an opportunity and that trial into a triumph.

Close your eyes, and do the head to toe relax and the Ten to One countdown, (these are described in Chapter 5 Finding Your Spiritual Self)

Now, visualize your self doing this thing, being successful and happy doing it and achieving it. See your self engaged in and enjoying the process and celebrating each step along the way. See and feel your self at the fruition of this goal, at the moment that you realize you have succeeded at and accomplished that which you were most fearful of, and spin those good feelings faster and stronger, and lock them in.

Now as you are feeling those powerful emotions of success, pride and accomplishment spin them into the process. See each step along the way and spin your joy and fulfillment into the process, into each step along the way, as you lock those good feelings in and connect them to each and every step and effort.

After you come out of meditation and open your eyes, write down all the steps, or the first few steps, that would get you closer to doing this thing and then, link back to your feelings of success and look at those first few steps.

Which one are you ready to take now?

Write it down. I'm patient. I'll wait. Skip to the end of the chapter and write out the first few steps you could take and which one you are ready to take right now.

If you are having trouble, that's okay, get a partner to help you in doing this thing. Choose a close friend who you can explain your fear to, who you can describe your plan of action to, and who can hold you accountable for taking each step.

Take that first step and don't worry about the results or other people's reactions. Some people might not like this new change, they may feel challenged by it or afraid of it, so don't worry about how they respond to it. Instead focus on nothing else but succeeding at your desire, at using this challenge to make you better not bitter. Once you have overcome your greatest obstacle, one you have succeeded at your toughest challenge, you will be that better self you have been dreaming of becoming.

I remember training with Dr. Richard Bandler at a Neuro-Linguistic Programming seminar where he was curing phobias. A young lady made her way up onto the stage and admitted that she had been suffering from debilitating claustrophobia for over a decade. She could not ride in small cars, subways or even airplanes and had a room on the first floor of the hotel because elevators were way too small for her to take. She shared with Dr. Bandler that her dream was to be able to visit the water parks in Florida, where the training was being held, and slide down the water slides, but she was too afraid to go into the small tubes.

Before putting her into a hypnotic trance, Dr. Bandler told her that after he worked with her he was going to lock her in a small, dark equipment closet at the back of the seminar room. The look of fear on her face was overwhelming. A few minutes later, after hypnotizing her and running her through a few NLP strategies, Dr. Bandler brought her out of trance and asked her to walk to the back of the room and go into the closet. She walked calmly, smiling all the way, entered the tiny closet and turned around to face us. As Dr.

Bandler shut the door, we could see her standing there, with a huge smile on her face.

About twenty minutes later, after working with a different seminar participant, Dr. Bandler opened the closet door, and there she stood, still smiling. As she walked out of the closet Dr. Bandler looked her in the eye and said "Now, the most important thing for you to know is that if you can do that, you can do anything you want for the rest of your life and that is the best feeling in the world."

Later that day she rode in the hotel's elevator just for fun and the next day she visited the water parks, rode on the slides and had the time of her life.

The same is true for you. Once you have confronted your greatest fear and overcome it, you will realize that there is nothing in this world that you cannot do and that is the greatest feeling on earth! And you will have that feeling once you Find Your Better Self.

Finding Your Better Self
ACTIONS TO TAKE

1. Write down that one thing that you know you should quit doing, or start doing, that one thing that you are most afraid of.

One Thing I Can Stop Doing:

_____

_____

_____

One Thing I Can Start Doing:

_____

_____

_____

2. Write out a story of you taking action on that issue and it going better than you could have imagined.

This is the Story of how I successfully stopped and how it changed my life.

_____

_____

_____

_____

_____

_____

_____

This is the Story of how I successfully started and how it changed my life.

_____

_____

_____

_____

_____

_____

_____

_____

_____

_____

_____

_____

_____

_____

_____

_____

_____

_____

_____

3. Write down a few steps you can take to help you stop and what your first step will be.

The first few steps I can take are:

_____

_____

_____

_____

_____

_____

_____

_____

_____

_____

The step I am ready to take now is:

_____

_____

_____

_____

_____

_____

_____

Write down a few steps you can take to help you get started and what your first step will be.

_____

_____

_____

_____

_____

_____

_____

_____

The step I am ready to take now is:

_____

_____

_____

_____

_____

_____

4. Get a partner if you want help to keep you accountable and each day visualize your self succeeding at your challenge.

People who could be my accountability partner:

_____

_____

_____

_____

09 | FIND YOUR SELF AMONG OTHERS

My backpacking buddy, Tim, and I were on a winter snow-shoeing trip in the Sierra Nevada when we had an unexpected encounter.

Tim and I had known each other and camped together for years. We both loved the rugged beauty of the wilderness and the solitude of being in the backcountry alone. We could roll into camp after a long day on the trail and have the tent pitched, water boiling on the fire, and camp made without even saying a word to each other. We knew each other and each other's patterns that well.

On this particular trip, we had planned to snow-shoe a few miles to the Peter Grubb Hut, a backcountry wilderness hut maintained by the Sierra Club. Since it was in the middle of winter, on a weekday, we planned to have the place, and the solitude, all to ourselves. We crunched over the snowpack and through the cold silence for hours, eventually coming to the hut as evening was beginning to settle over the land. When we first spied smoke coming out of the hut's chimney, and a yellow glow of light, beaming out of its windows and onto the snow, we were disappointed to realize we wouldn't be alone.

As we opened the thick wooden door of the cabin, we were greeted with the warmth and glow of a fire and the raucous sounds of music and laughter. We spent the night laughing, singing and drinking with our new friends: three cross-country skiers who were on holiday from Germany and the Netherlands, and a husband and wife pair, from California. They had guitars, wine, great food and even better stories. Even though we were looking for solitude, it ended up being one of our favorite backcountry memories, because of the people we met along the way.

Studies have shown that we become like the five people we spend the most time around. We become like them in many ways: We rise or fall to their income level, adopt their interests and tastes, and even begin speaking and acting like them.

So, it is vitally important if you want to find your true self, who you really are, that you take a good look at who you are spending the most time around and who you would like to spend more time with than you already are.

Are there people or groups that you are involved with that no longer serve you? Are there places you go and people you hang out with that don't seem to be a good fit for you anymore, or that no longer make you happy?

Are there people in your life that you haven't been spending much time with? Are their old friends, family members, groups or organizations that you used to spend time with, who you used to enjoy?

Make a list of those people and groups who you would like to spend more time with and those who it would be better if you had less time together.

First, start with the individuals, the people, you would enjoy having in your life more. Some of these might be people who live near you, folks who you can have a cup of tea with, take a walk with, go to lunch or a movie together, go golfing or shopping, or whatever. Other folks on your list may live far away, but you can still resolve to call them more often, to talk on a regular basis, and then to visit them or have them visit you.

Some of these people might be very close to you, people that you see each and every day: Your own spouse or partner, your kids, parents and co-workers. Perhaps you would like more quality time with your partner or children, or maybe you would enjoy spending time with your colleagues outside of work?

The only question that matters is: Who would you like to have more quality time with now?

Go ahead and begin your list now. Write down those first names that come to mind and underneath each person's name, list a few things you would both enjoy doing together.

Go ahead. I'll wait. I'm patient. Skip to the end of the chapter and get started on your list.

Now that you have your list started, make a firm decision to contact the people on your list and invite them to do something together. Remember, they may, like you, also be stuck in a rut, and it may be difficult for them, at first, to break their routine and make the time to get together. So, don't worry about rejections and be persistent. Be the leader in the relationship and make your time together happen.

Enjoy that long phone conversation and then don't wait a few weeks or months to call that friend or family member again. Do it soon. Do it often.

Enjoy that lunch date with your friend, or that hike in nature, or enjoy having that friend over to watch a movie or listen to music or do whatever. And then, don't wait a few weeks or months to get together again. Do it soon. Do it often.

Notice which friends and activities are the most fun and fulfilling for you. Pay attention to how each makes you feel and pursue those friendships you are enjoying the most.

Next, make a list of those groups and organizations you used to participate in or might like to join. Perhaps it's a church group, or a group of volunteers in your church, or maybe it's a local organization like the Sierra or Rotary Club, or a book club, or sewing circle. You might volunteer at the food pantry, soup kitchen or local school, or you might join a choir or athletic club. Look for groups of people who are like-minded to you and groups that are involved in areas of interest that you share.

Go ahead and begin your list now. Write down a few of those groups that you are thinking of right now that you might join.

Go ahead. I'll wait. I'm patient. Skip to the end of the chapter and do it. Write Now.

Do some research on what groups there are in your area that share your interests.

Groups like this often add a second element that is helpful in finding our selves. In addition to communion with others, they often provide a purpose, something for us to care about and believe in. Whether it's helping those in need or trying to improve our bowling score, when we are striving for a purpose we are always happier and more fulfilled than when we are not.

This is one way that you can find your self among others. You can find a purpose through other people, a cause to join, something even greater than you are as an individual that you can be a part of.

This was the case for Joan de Arc, George Washington, Martin Luther King, Saint Theresa and every other person who changed history. They did not do it alone. They were part of something. Whether a leader or a follower they were part of a larger cause, part of a group with a similar belief system.

This is the truth of all religions, cults, athletic teams, successful businesses, intact communities, close knit families and happy individuals. In each instance, each individual member feels that they belong and that they matter, and that what they do matters, and thus they have purpose and that purpose has meaning and that meaning has connection and that connection has certainty and that feels really, really good.

So make a firm decision now to attend one or several of their meetings, and when you do, make a concerted effort to introduce your self to others, to meet as many people in the group as you can. Work to join the group and get to know its members right away and give your self and the group several chances before you decide whether to keep it on your Friend List permanently or not.

You can also make your own groups and circles. For one summer I lived in a tent in the woods outside Ketchikan, Alaska and worked in restaurants washing dishes to save up money for college. When I wasn't working, I spent a lot of time hanging out in the local coffee shop where they had several chess boards. So, I set up a Chess group, simply by putting up a hand written flier and telling the baristas that every Tuesday and Thursday at 2:00 I would be there to play chess with anyone who wanted to. After a few weeks, we had a small group of regulars who would show up to play, watch others play, and talk and laugh. Our group ranged from college-aged men and women like me to a boy in junior high school (who could beat almost all of us all the time) and several elderly men and women. It was a diverse and fun group and we really got to know and enjoy each other's company whether we were playing chess or not.

Similarly, I once read a story about a retired woman who moved into an apartment in a new building and was feeling lonely because she didn't know any of her neighbors. She posted a notice that on one afternoon each week she would open her apartment for anyone to come visit and have tea and listen to classical music. Her group started slowly, with just one person visiting at first, and then it began to grow. Soon, you could find a small group of neighbors in her apartment chatting like old friends and sharing their favorite composers and pieces of classical music on a regular basis.

So, whether your group already exists or not, you can find or make one to join.

Go ahead, start making a list now. What are some things that you enjoy doing? What are some activities that you enjoy that you could form a group around, or find a group to join? And who could you invite to join that group or activity?

Perhaps you will start a book club, or poker group. Maybe you will start a group for artists to get together, or find a work-out or hiking partner or group. Whatever subject you are interested in is a perfect subject for collecting like-minded people who you will enjoy.

Go ahead and start on your list. Skip to the end of the chapter and write down a few ideas.

You now have Three Lists.

1. A list of people who you would like to spend more time with.

2. A list of groups you might like to join.

3. A list of activities around which you could form a group.

Let's create one final list, a shadow list, a list of who and what you should get rid of. Are there any people or groups that you spend time with who longer serve you?

It's okay if they were very important to you at one time in your life. The question is whether or not they are a good fit for you now. Does spending time with them feel like an obligation? Has it become unpleasant or unfulfilling for you? Or is that person or group bad for you? Are they stunting your growth, encouraging your bad habits or dragging you down?

Ask your self this one, simple question: Would the best version of my self that I can imagine continue to spend time with them? If the answer is "probably not," then put them on your list and start removing them from your life.

You see it's important to realize this is Your life, nobody else's. No one is going to live it for you. So, if someone is no longer a good fit for you, set them free and free your self from their influence.

Go ahead and skip to #4 at the end of this chapter and write down the people, places and groups your best self wants to avoid.

As soon as you cut these people out of your life you will have space and time to fill up with the people who you truly want to be with and benefit from being around. Instead of being pulled down by negative people, you will feel your self lifted up by those who connect with your truest self and highest good.

Now, make a powerful decision that you will make an effort each and every week to engage with some of the people and groups on your lists. Choose those you are most drawn to and that seem easiest at first and then work down your list adding in more people and activities as you go.

In this way you are expanding the boundaries of your life, expanding the size of your tribe, and increasing the opportunities for you to Find Your Self Among Others.

Finding Your Self Among Others
ACTIONS TO TAKE

1. Make a list of people who you would like to spend more time with, a list of friends and family members whose company you enjoy.

People who I can spend more time with:

_____

_____

_____

_____

_____

_____

_____

_____

_____

_____

_____

2. Make a list of groups you can join or create of like-minded people doing things you enjoy.

Groups I could join or create:

_____

_____

_____

_____

_____

_____

_____

_____

_____

_____

_____

_____

_____

_____

_____

_____

_____

_____

3. Make a powerful decision to be the leader and invite these people to do things with you and to join them in what they do. And pay attention to how you feel while you're doing it, so you know who to add to your list and who to take off.

Things I could Invite others to do with me and/or people I could invite:

_____

_____

_____

_____

_____

_____

_____

_____

_____

_____

_____

_____

_____

4. Are there any people, places, or groups that you should stop spending time with or spend less time with? If so, write them down here.

People, places and groups to avoid:

_____

_____

_____

_____

_____

_____

_____

_____

_____

_____

_____

10 | FIND YOUR SELF ALONE

It's easy to get lost in others, to follow the wrong people, to get sidetracked or put on the wrong path. This is especially true when many of the people around us are lost in their own lives, and when the ones who have found themselves aren't going in the same direction we're heading in anyway.

I've had students who were so busy talking as they hiked that they walked right on past camp, or followed whoever was in the lead so blindly that they missed the fork in the trail and hiked on for miles in the wrong direction. This has happened on more than one occasion and just goes to show you how easily we get lost in the influence of others.

I remember one time when I was leading a group of university students on a week-long backpacking trip and we were base-camped at a beautiful mountain lake at the foot of a peak. Our plan for the day was to climb the peak together, return to base-camp and resume backpacking the next day. On our way to the summit from base-camp we passed a place where another trail joined ours. I stopped the group and pointed it out to them, emphasizing that when we came back down the mountain this would look like a fork in the trail and it would be easy to go the wrong way.

"So, remember," I said, "If you are returning to camp without me, when you get to this fork, you must stay to the right. If you go left,

89

it will take you into a completely different valley than the one we are camped in, on the opposite side of this mountain." I even made an arrow out of stones on the ground pointing to the right and made sure everyone looked closely at it.

A few hours later, after summiting the peak and enjoying the views from the top, a few people wanted to return to camp early. I reminded them to all stay together and to look for the arrow and the fork in the trail and to make sure they stayed to the right. Of course, they were so busy talking and walking quickly downhill that they blew right by the fork without ever seeing it and took the trail to the left, into a valley they had never been in before, and where their camp and camping gear were absent.

When we made it back to base-camp and saw that they weren't there, I knew immediately what happened. Taking an experienced hiking partner with me, we went back up from base camp, took the left trail and caught up with them many miles and hours later. By the time we found them, it was getting dark and they were sitting next to the trail, aware of their mistake and completely demoralized. Fortunately, we had brought extra water, snacks and headlamps and were able to lead them safely back to base-camp.

Hiking alone, I doubt any one of them would have missed the trail, but caught up in their conversations with others and following along with the group, they very easily lost their way.

In your own life there may have been times when you got in with the wrong crowd, or lost some part of your self to a bad relationship or job. Right now there might be things and people that are distracting you from what you really want to be and do.

Even if these distractions are pleasant, they can become overwhelming, if you don't get a break from them every now and then. This is especially true if they have been leading you around in dizzy circles and keeping you from finding your self for quite some time.

First, in order to find your self or center your self, you need to know that you are the center.

You are the center of Your Universe.

But you are not the center of The Universe.

Everyone is the center of Their Universe.

The Universe is multi-centered because it is a Multi-verse.

This is why finding your self, finding the center of your world, is so important. This is also why you have to do it for your self. Nobody can find your center for you.

You must realize the paradoxical truth that in Your Universe, you are the center, the still point around which everything turns, and everyone and everything else is just passing through, for your benefit, while at the same time, in everyone else's Universe, they are each the center, and you are just passing through for their benefit.

Each one of us is the center, the center of our own world.

So, in this Finding Your Self Alone exercise you are going to take some time to explore that center, by making a list of activities that you can do alone.

You might want to focus on those things that you often do with others and to engage in a little experiment and try doing them by your self. Go to lunch or a movie by your self, or shopping, or to a sporting or artistic event. You might want to plan a short solo vacation, or an evening to cook a meal and listen to music at home alone.

After graduating with my Bachelors, I moved to Mexico to teach in an elementary school in a small pueblo on the Yucatan peninsula.

When that job ended, I spent the next few months by myself taking buses and hitch-hiking all over Mexico, Belize and Guatemala.

Although I met many people on my travels, I spent a lot of time alone. I camped in and explored the Coscomb Jaguar Sanctuary in Belize, and although I found the old wreckage of an airplane in the jungle, I didn't see another human being for a week. I hitch-hiked along roads where you only saw one car every few hours, and it was a logging or mango truck, where they made you ride in the back. I hid out in Tikal when the park closed and spent the night by myself on top of a pyramid. I pitched my hammock and mosquito net in the jungle alongside the road in between towns when I couldn't get a ride. I woke up in cabanas and motel rooms groggy from sleep and not knowing for a few minutes what city or country I was in. I shopped in mercados, ate in restaurants and drank in bars, and always I was alone.

It was truly a great time. I was always alone, but I was never lonely. I can still recall that I would spend hours, walking or riding along, humming the chorus from a song called *"Circle"* by Edie Brickell and the New Bohemians, which was popular at the time:

> "And being alone
> Is the best way to be.
> When I'm by myself it's
> The best way to be.
> When I'm all alone it's
> The best way to be."

Developing the ability to be comfortable with your self and to be confident doing things alone is an essential skill in life. Think about it.

Who is the one person who is always with you?

Who is that one person involved in everything you do?

Who goes everywhere you go?

Who talks to everyone you talk to?

Who is always there talking in your head, even when you are all alone?

You, that's who. And since you are always going to follow your self around, you probably better make really good friends with your self. And that means spending some quality time alone together.

In order to find your self alone, you need to spend time doing things on your own, by your self.

What are those things you often do with others that you could try doing alone? Take your self out on a date and get a nice dinner and take in a movie or a play. Or maybe you will go to a concert by your self, or to the beach, zoo or museum. You might find that you will have a really good time going camping, playing golf or basketball by your self. If you often practice Yoga or Martial Arts in a classroom setting, or sing in a choir with others, try that activity by your self and see how you like it.

Go ahead and skip to the back of the chapter now to get started on your list. What can you try doing alone?

Go ahead. I'll wait. I'm patient. Write on your list now.

Now that you have your first list started, think about things that you have enjoyed doing alone in the past like getting a massage, taking a nap or long bath, or reading or drawing.

Are there things you enjoy, or used to enjoy, doing alone that you haven't done for awhile? Perhaps it's meditating or gardening, lifting weights, hiking or walking. What activities do you do alone that you could enjoy doing more often? Writing, baking, painting, woodworking, etc.

Skip to the end of the chapter now and get started on this list of activities that you already know you enjoy doing by your self.

Go ahead. I'll wait. I'm patient. Write on your list now.

Then there are other things that you might do for your self alone, such as cleaning your house or bedroom, or organizing the tools in the garage, or the files or pictures on your computer. You might go through your closet and donate all the old clothes you no longer wear so you have room for some new ones. You might go through family pictures and make a photo album or shutterfly book. Or perhaps you've been putting off cleaning out the fridge or your car and it would feel really good to get that accomplished.

What are some things you can do for your self and by your self that you will enjoy doing or that you will enjoy having done?

As you try out these new activities by your self, spend some time journaling about your experiences. Write about the different things you are doing by your self and how you feel about them. Write about who you are, what you value, and who you care about. Write about where you've come from and where you would like to go. Write about what you think and how you feel, about your self, your world, and your place in it. Write about whatever you want.

It's important to know, as you do this, that spending time by your self does not take anything away from the other people in your life. That's not how self-development works. By spending time on your self, by fueling your self up first, you are actually making sure you have more to give to others.

Imagine that you are an island in the middle of the ocean and you begin growing and getting larger. You are not stealing any water from the ocean. You are not taking anything away from the ocean by enlarging your self. In fact, what you are doing is actually increasing your circumference, increasing the length of your shoreline. And that means you are giving the ocean more opportunities to come into contact with you, more ways to get to know who you really are.

So, grow large and find Your Self Alone so that the ocean of life may get to know who you really are.

Finding Your Self Alone
ACTIONS TO TAKE

1. Take some time to do some things you enjoy, and might normally do with others, all by your self. (eating out, going to a movie, taking a short trip or a long bath)

Things I could try doing alone:

_____

_____

_____

_____

_____

_____

_____

_____

2. Write down things that you already know you enjoy doing by your self that you could do more often.

Things I enjoy doing alone:

_____

_____

_____

_____

_____

_____

_____

_____

_____

3. Do some work for your self alone (housework, organizing your office, closet, garage or computer files).

Things I can do for myself alone:

_____

_____

_____

_____

_____

_____

4. Journal about the experiences and which ones you enjoyed and want to do more of, and which ones you want to invite others to join you in doing.

Favorite things to do alone:

_____

_____

_____

_____

_____

_____

_____

11 | FIND YOUR PAST SELF

One way of finding your self again if you are lost in the wilderness is called backtracking. First you trace back your steps in your memory, noting how many ridges you crossed, which landmarks you passed and so on. Then, you turn around and begin searching for your previous footprints. Find and discover your trail, noting what your boot tracks look like, how far apart they are and so on. Then follow this trail, as if you were tracking an outlaw in the wilderness, step by step, each step of the way until you make it back to landmarks you recognize.

Sometimes the best way to find out where you are is to look at where you have been.

My dad and I were backpacking in the Colorado Rockies one summer and had base-camped near two fourteen thousand foot peaks we planned to climb. We had a nice day climbing and summited easily, but soon found ourselves enshrouded in fog, as a huge bank of clouds suddenly blew in, around and under us. Just a few minutes before, we had 360 degree views all around. We were looking down into the mountain valleys on both sides and could easily see which one of the many ridges we had followed up to the summit. Now, however, we could only see the ground about five feet in front of our faces. The clouds were so thick that if we got more than a few feet away from each other we completely disappeared from each other's sight in the fog.

Although we knew the general direction back to base camp, there were multiple ridges leading that direction, only one of which would actually take us into the correct drainage. The wrong ridge would lead us far astray, take us away from our survival gear and get us hopelessly lost. In addition, we were so enshrouded by the clouds that we couldn't even see the sun and the dizzying and disorienting fog made us question even our general sense of direction.

It was clear that the peak was going to be socked in for many hours, if not days, and we couldn't wait for the weather to clear. The fog was wet, it was getting cold and we needed to find our camp and gear before nightfall or we would be in a desperate situation. So, without the ability to look for familiar landmarks and only a few feet of visibility we had no choice but to study the ground. We traced our steps carefully, making note of the fresh print of one of our boots in the dirt in between rocks, or where we had sheltered under a large boulder from the wind, or where I accidentally dropped a tiny piece of orange peel. After some time of this painstaking progress, we dropped down out of the clouds and could begin to make out the valley below us. We were relieved to see that we were in the right valley, our camp lay below us and we had successfully backtracked off the peak to safety.

Sometimes in life, and in the wilderness, you aren't looking for where you have just been, but instead you are looking for where you were a long time ago. We can get lost in time just as easily as we can get lost in space.

When my brother and I were teenagers we explored all kinds of caves and mines throughout Colorado and Wyoming. Near my Grandmother's house, which we visited each summer, we made our greatest discovery: a large cave, over half a mile long, with the tiniest and most unobtrusive of openings. You actually had to belly crawl for the first twenty feet to get into the cave, then it opened up into a tunnel of massive proportions.

Three decades later, after both my brother and grandmother had passed, my cousin and I were visiting Wyoming to scatter Grandma

Dot's ashes, and share with our teenage children the places where we grew up. My cousin, Michelle, and I were taking our kids to all of our favorite childhood playgrounds from 30 years earlier.

I wanted to give my nieces and nephews, and my own kids, a taste of the adventures Bart and I had, so we made a plan to go and look for the cave. We easily found the cliff face where the cave was located and began climbing and crawling all around looking for its hidden opening.

FIELD NOTES

Whether you are looking for your past self from yesterday or yesteryear, you can find them and bring them back with you to the present.

After a number of failed attempts to find the opening, I stopped exploring physically and sat down to explore my memories. A few minutes later I could see the opening in my mind, a weird "S" shape and a narrow tunnel that looked like a dead end. With a clear picture now in my mind, I returned to the cliff face and soon we found the jackpot. We crawled out of the hot summer sun and into the cool darkness of the cave, and as its roof and walls opened up, I got to see my kids' faces light up in wonder, just as mine and Bart's had so many years before. In that moment, I knew we had returned home.

Even though he passed away years earlier, Bart, Michelle and I were home again, exploring the wildlands of Wyoming together, and this time with our children.

Right now, you may feel lost in the fog of time. You may feel like you have lost some part of your self. And whether you want to trace your steps back into the recent past, or travel across the years into your more distant past, you can find that past self, who is still with you today.

Whether you are looking for your past self from yesterday or yesteryear, you can find them and bring them back with you to the present. They haven't ever gone anywhere. They've always been right here, waiting for you to find them and invite them on your journey with you, if you want.

Your present self, the one that is wandering around aimlessly lost, is the sum total of all of your past experiences. By tracing back through your past and examining who you were and how you changed at different times in your life, you can discover much about who you are today and how you came to be here, now.

You may discover forgotten memories, treasures you dropped along the way, and decide to pick them up again. You may also see things you threw away on purpose and decide to leave them where they belong, in the past, behind you. As you do this, you will get to see the many different and varied forms of your self that you have been in the past.

When you have been lost in the wilderness for some time and have been tracing your steps backward, I can tell you that there is a great and comfortable feeling, like coming home again, when you finally recognize that first landmark and remember where you are.

It is exactly the same feeling when you find, recognize and step into Your Past Self again.

It's like waking up at 5:00 in the morning, before the alarm clock, as if it were Christmas morning and it's just an ordinary day, and you are so brimming with excitement that you can't wait to be you! So, let's recapture some of that childhood wonder and take a trip through time into your past.

Divide your life into 5 or 10 year chunks of time, and review each one in your journal. At the end of this chapter I have divided life into decades with some blank spaces for you to get started. Write about where you lived, what you did, what you were like, what you liked doing, what you hated, and so on. Go through past pictures of your childhood, early adulthood, and adulthood to help you recall specific memories. Enjoy and savor this process and everything that you remember.

You might want to make a picture and story album of favorite moments in your past to relive and enjoy. Maybe you will start writing an autobiography or a fictional novel about your past life.

In order to get started, skip to the end of the chapter and begin writing out your lists. Go ahead. I'll wait. I'm patient. Write now.

First, think back to when you were very little. What were you interested in when you were under 10 years of age? Sometimes it helps to recall where you lived or went to school, during those early years.

List some things you liked when you were a little kid. What were your favorite toys, games to play, books, movies, teachers, subjects?

What are some of your favorite memories?

Now, list some things that you liked when you were 10-20 years of age?

List what you were into when you were a teenager. What did you like to do in high school and college? What kinds of hobbies did you have, what books, movies, and music did you like?

Now, what did you enjoy when you were 20-30 years of age?

List some things you liked doing in your twenties. Who did you spend time with? Where did you live? What did you like to do? What kinds of things were you involved in? What are your favorite memories?

And, what did you enjoy when you were 30-40?

List some things you liked doing when you were in your thirties. Where were you living? Did you have children or a career to focus on? What other things were important to you?

Continue to make a list for each decade of your life up to the present that describes your favorite memories, your past hobbies, enjoyable activities and interests.

Now, as you review this list ask your self how can you engage in these things, or things similar to them, now, at this age?

You don't have to engage with that activity in exactly the same way now, as you used to, so be flexible in how you approach it. I still love Tae Kwon Do, for example, just as much as I did when I started at 11 and when I competed at the Olympic level in my twenties, but I don't do it the same way. I don't compete in Tae Kwon Do anymore, but I do teach more, and still enjoy practicing. So, whatever the activity is, ask your self how you could experience that side of Your Self today.

When I was younger I bow-hunted, fished, took long camping trips, practiced wilderness survival techniques and loved being outdoors. Today I still love being outdoors. I just engage with the activity in different ways. I don't hunt anymore, for example. Now I spend more time just watching wildlife, identifying wild plants, hiking and taking shorter camping trips. I still get to enjoy this lifelong passion of mine, especially because I've allowed my relationship with that passion to change.

You might decide, for example, that your love of dinosaurs when you were seven years old is not an abiding passion or topic of interest as an adult and you may not want to pursue it. Or, you might decide that your love of natural history could be experienced and enjoyed by volunteering to become a docent at the zoo or museum and to help lead tours.

Or if you loved playing make believe in the woods as a little kid, you could join a Live Action Role Play group and do exactly that. Or you could find a fantasy adventure series to read or watch, or you could start hiking in the woods and studying native plants and flowers. Depending on what it was that you enjoyed about that activity, find some way to engage with that passion today and Find Your Past Self and bring them with you back to the present.

Finding Your Past Self
ACTIONS TO TAKE

1. Go through old pictures and keepsakes, or simply reflect upon your own memories of your childhood and past, and write about what you were interested in and liked to do at different ages. Things I liked 1 to 10 years of age:

_____

_____

_____

_____

_____

Things I liked 10 to 20 years of age:

_____

_____

_____

_____

_____

_____

_____

_____

_____

_____

_____

Things I liked 20 to 30 years of age:

_____

_____

_____

_____

_____

_____

_____

_____

_____

_____

_____

Things I liked 30 to 40 years of age:

_____

_____

_____

_____

_____

_____

_____

_____

_____

Things I liked 40 to 50 years of age:

_____

_____

_____

_____

_____

_____

Things I liked 50 to 60 years of age:

_____

_____

_____

_____

_____

Things I liked 60 to 70 years of age:

_____

_____

_____

_____

_____

Things I liked 70 to 80 years of age:

_____

_____

_____

_____

2. Review these journals and come up with a list of things from your past that you might like to do, or learn about, or be involved in again.

Things from my past that I might like to do again:

_____

_____

_____

_____

_____

_____

_____

_____

_____

_____

_____

_____

_____

_____

3. Take action on these activities and make note of which ones you want to continue to pursue.

12 | FIND YOUR PRESENT SELF

Sometimes the best way to respond, once you realize you are lost, is not to go charging off in search of landmarks or the way home. Quite often your best option is to find a good spot to make shelter and hunker down where you are. This means embracing the present place and moment, noting what shelter and fire materials are near at hand and making home in the here and now. In order to do this, you have to look around and memorize your surroundings, and learn to call them Home and Here, and then you work to improve them and you appreciate your work.

If hiking out means that you will risk hypothermia or heat stroke, or that you may become more lost or injured because of rugged terrain, the best option may be to stay put. This is especially true if someone knows where you went and when you should return and can alert authorities when you are missed.

One of my Tae Kwon Do students, a young teen, was on a backpacking trip with his grandfather when they realized they had gotten lost. In the exceptionally rugged mountains of the Northern California this is easy. They had accidentally taken a wrong trail, which turned into a game trail, which eventually disappeared completely, leaving them with the realization that they didn't really know the way back. After some attempts to backtrack and find a familiar landmark and the grandfather twisting his knee, they decided to make camp and wait for rescue.

Three days later, search and rescue found them, safe and warm, well hydrated and very hungry. Although they had very little to eat for those three days, they had a fire and shelter, sleeping bags and water. By embracing their present situation, rather than resisting it, they were able to wait comfortably for help, rather than risk life and limb in the rugged terrain.

My student said he actually enjoyed the time he spent with his grandpa because he felt safe the entire time. They had tea and hot chocolate at night, rationed their food, played cards, talked and simply waited for help to arrive.

There are times in our lives too, when it would be wise to slow down and not rush in to change or fix things. There are times when we can lose ourselves in regretting the past, or being afraid of, or planning too much for, the future. These are times when learning how to be present is truly a gift.

This is how you Find Your Present Self. You start right where you are: Here and Now. You start by embracing the Here and Now and truly appreciating it, without trying to change it.

When I was 18, I spent a summer living in a tent in the woods outside Ketchikan, Alaska and washed dishes to save up money for college. I picked blueberries in the morning alongside black bears and ate them on my granola and in the evening I ate steak and crab leftovers and washed the plates of rich tourists who were as fat as the bears. I had nothing and I loved it!

I loved every minute of it! I loved waking up to banana slugs on the outside of my tent, the damp, musty smell of my sleeping bag, and the weekly shower I got at the hotel for free. I loved standing in line at the soup kitchen and eating at the long tables, spending rainy afternoons in the coffee shop nursing a bottomless cup of coffee and walking the docks looking for odd jobs.

It was tough. I didn't have much and I loved it.

That's what it means to be present and grateful.

You might have a lot, you might have it all, or you might have very little, that doesn't matter. What matters is whether or not you enjoy it, appreciate it, and are grateful for it.

During another great chapter of my life I lived with my dear friend and mentor, Master James Craeton, in a small house on the back of our instructor's property. GrandMaster Yi let us both live there rent free as payment for teaching some of the Tae Kwon Do classes at his academy. It was a shitty old concrete block house with a rusted tin roof, so we called it the "Love shack" after the song, you know, "tin roof, rusted." Anyway, for the first year that we lived there, like monks, we had no running water and went out into the woods with a shovel to go to the bathroom. We had black belt bonfire parties where we broke flaming logs with kicks and hand strikes and swam in the farm pond, and trained and trained, and talked about training, and trained more, and had absolutely nothing, and we were so happy, and so present.

We knew that what we were doing was a deep and meaningful part of ourselves and that it wouldn't last, and that we better enjoy it and embrace it. We were so present that we thought very little about our future. It was as if we were suspended in a timeless present that was so wonderful we could have enjoyed it for decades, and yet we still knew it wouldn't last forever, and that knowledge made us appreciate it even more.

So, how do you enjoy and embrace your present life? How do you get more enjoyment out of who you are experiencing being and expressing as your self right now? How can you be more of your Present Self and enjoy your present self more now?

The first practice, to enjoy your present self more now is to begin and continue a daily gratitude practice. Each day, I recommend you do it in the morning, write out 10 things you are grateful for in your life. You can start each gratitude with the simple phrase "I am so happy and grateful for..." And when you write out the gratitude statement make sure to really feel those feelings of appreciation. Your gratitude list may contain many of the same things each day and you can add in different things as you think of them or experience them. My wife and kids, for example, are on my gratitude list almost every single day. Sometimes I will include things on my gratitude list that have not happened yet but that I am hoping to make happen. For example, I might write that "I am so happy and grateful that I have finished writing the *Field Guide to Finding Your Self* and it is published and selling off the shelves in avalanches." Even when I still had several chapters to write, that gratitude helped connect me to the joy I would feel when I completed the project.

As you interact with the people, things and activities on your gratitude list remind your self how much you appreciate them and really savor their presence in your life. Give compliments and appreciations to those people who are on your list and give thanks for even the simple things in your life.

For example, try for one day to note all the miraculous wonders and comforts and riches in your world. Does water come out when you turn on the faucet? Do the lights magically come on when you flick the switch? Is there food to eat in your kitchen? Do you have a soft, warm bed to sleep on? Are you able to read this?

Wow! What miracles? From a wilderness survival perspective— or from the lived experience of millions of people on the planet— to have any one of these things would be a miraculous change in their lives.

Notice, marvel at, and appreciate all the daily miracles around you. This helps you to maintain your awareness of, and appreciation for, all the blessings you do have so that you can enjoy them even more. Once you have found Your Present Self, right where you are, and started to really appreciate everything you have, you can also work to improve it.

Once you decide to wait for rescue, you immediately work to memorize your surroundings and improve them. You build a shelter and collect firewood for a fire. You find a water source and a way to signal for rescue. You come to love and appreciate your new little home for as long as you are there.

In the same way, you can ask how to improve your present while appreciating it. For everything on your gratitude list ask "what can I do to enjoy that thing, person, or experience more?"

Notice what things you are grateful for in your present reality and then ask your self how can I enjoy or appreciate or experience that thing more fully? If you enjoy getting a massage or going for a hike, ask your self if you are doing these things often enough.

If your partner or children show up on your gratitude list often, for example, you can ask your self "what would I enjoy doing with them, or for them?"

Or, you might give your self the gift of cleaning your car out, decorating the house, organizing your closet or garage, or anything else that will help you to enjoy your present space, the here and now, just a little bit more.

So take some time to look around your life, right here and now, and find what you enjoy and appreciate about this wonderful gift called Your Present Self.

As they say, Yesterday is history, tomorrow is mystery, and today is a gift. That's why they call it "The Present."

Unwrap and appreciate the present gift of your life each day by making note of and appreciating all those things you are grateful for. Whether those miracles are big or small, make your life richer by taking the time to appreciate, celebrate and savor them.

Finding Your Present Self
ACTIONS TO TAKE

1. Every Day make a list of Ten things (people, experiences, objects, situations, etc.) about your present life that you are grateful for. You can begin these sentences with "I am so happy and grateful now that....." Do this for 40 days or more.

My First Gratitude List for today is:

1. _____

_____

_____

2. _____

_____

_____

3. _____

_____

_____

4. _____

_____

_____

5. _____

_____

_____

6. _____

_____

_____

7. _____

_____

_____

8. _____

_____

_____

9. _____

_____

_____

10. _____

_____

_____

(to be continued in your journal each and every day by you)

2. Make a gratitude list of things and people you appreciate and want to enjoy more, and how you might enjoy and appreciate them more.

Things and people I want to enjoy more:

_____

_____

_____

_____

_____

_____

_____

_____

_____

_____

_____

_____

_____

_____

_____

_____

_____

_____

_____

_____

_____

_____

_____

_____

3. Each day when you are interacting with those people and doing those things you appreciate, make sure to savor those moments, and compliment those people, and say a gratitude for them in your mind.

13 | FIND YOUR FUTURE SELF

In many mountainous regions, if you become lost the best course of action is simply to walk downhill. Walking downhill is easier, takes less energy and is less dangerous, than traversing up and down ridges, across country. If you start walking downhill, eventually you will hit a stream or drainage which you can follow downhill and eventually it will hit a larger stream or river for you to follow downhill. Since we build our roads and houses and cities along rivers, this will eventually lead you back to civilization.

One winter after recently learning how to snowboard I went with a friend backcountry snowshoeing and boarding and we got completely lost. Our plan was to climb and traverse a ridge from the road, spend the afternoon making runs in some large snowfields and bowls and then drop back down through the trees to the road. However, at some point in the afternoon while enjoying the deep powder and trackless snow, we cruised down a slope that took us into the wrong drainage.

Once we realized our mistake we stopped and took stock of the situation. Unfortunately, since we were only planning on a day trip and thought we would be close to the road the whole time, we only had daypacks with minimal gear. Making a snow cave and sitting through the long cold night, fending off hypothermia, did not seem like the best option. In addition, since we had been boarding downhill for quite some time, the climb back up to the ridge, if we could find the right one and recognize a landmark, would take hours and we wouldn't make it there until dark. As we gauged the sunlight left and the hours of climbing required, the prospect of trudging along those ridgelines in the dark, looking for a familiar landmark, seemed both daunting and dangerous.

FIELD NOTES

When you look back on your life, what do you want to see that you have done, accomplished, experienced and left behind?

We had a general lay of the land, however, and we knew that the road we were looking for, wound down the mountain and around its base. So, if we simply went downhill, eventually we would hit the road we were looking for. We might be miles from our car but we would be safe. So we began carving our way through the deep powder, whizzing by trees and ducking branches as we made our way down the forested slope. After a while we found ourselves skiing down a snow-covered streambed which eventually ran directly under the road.

We shouldered our boards and clambered up onto the road happier than ever to see headlights and hear traffic. In a short while we hitched a ride and were soaking up the warmth from the heater, comfortably driving the miles back toward our car.

In many rugged and mountainous regions the best way to find your self is just like this, to act like water and just flow downhill, flow into being found. Sometimes when you are lost in the rugged wilderness of your life you can do the same thing and flow into your future, find your self by focusing on, and pouring your self into, your future. After all, that's the direction you are headed in anyway.

Let us imagine that many years from now, you are very old and lying on your deathbed, peacefully resting and waiting to cross over to the other side. As you lie there reflecting on your long and fruitful life, looking back on all the years, experiences and accomplishments what will you want to have done?

What do you want to do before you die?

_____

_____

_____

_____

_____

_____

_____

_____

_____

_____

_____

_____

_____

What kind of legacy do you want to leave?

_____

_____

_____

_____

_____

_____

_____

_____

_____

_____

_____

_____

_____

_____

_____

What do you want to experience or accomplish in this life?

_____

_____

_____

_____

_____

_____

_____

_____

_____

_____

_____

_____

_____

How do you want to be remembered and by who and for what?

_____

_____

_____

_____

_____

_____

_____

_____

What mark do you want to leave on the world?

_____

_____

_____

_____

_____

_____

_____

_____

_____

_____

_____

_____

_____

What contribution do you want to make?

_____

_____

_____

_____

_____

_____

_____

_____

_____

_____

_____

Do you want to leave your family an inheritance or property?
Do you want to help others, or create something that will last?

_____

_____

_____

_____

_____

_____

_____

Do you want to leave behind a story or a set of teachings?
Do you want your memory to live on in others you have touched?

_____

_____

_____

_____

_____

_____

_____

_____

Or is there something you want to have done or experienced before
you leave this planet?

_____

_____

_____

_____

_____

_____

_____

_____

_____

Is there a cause you want to join, a problem you want to solve?

_____

_____

_____

_____

When we are talking about leaving a legacy we are discussing two vital human needs: the need to have a purpose and the need to make a contribution. What is your purpose and contribution?

_____

_____

_____

_____

_____

_____

_____

_____

_____

Every human being on the planet, no matter how rich or poor, needs to have a purpose in life. As Viktor Frankl wrote in *Man's Search for Meaning* "Those who have a 'why' to live, can bear with almost any 'how'." Your purpose is your "why." Once you have developed a powerful purpose it will propel you through life and fulfill you along the way.

And when that purpose is larger than you, when it bleeds over into the lives of others, it becomes a legacy.

Legacies can be large or small. They can affect the life of one person or millions. It doesn't matter. Whether you write stories to entertain your grandchildren or novels to entertain millions doesn't matter.

The question is not how can you be remembered the longest, or how can you help the most people? It's not a competition, so "longest" and "most" don't matter.

The question is what do you want to be remembered for and what do you want to do in order to help others?

What unique part do you have to play? What unique gift do you have to give?

When you look back on your life, what do you want to see that you have done, accomplished, experienced and left behind?

Imagine that you are making an epic movie and it is titled "The Life of *(Insert your name here)*!" In this movie you are the star player. You are the hero. This movie might explore the obstacles you have overcome, the trials you have come through, and it will also explore the heroic journey you are on, the treasures and insights you bring back for others. This movie will detail your triumphs and successes. It will show your peak moments and greatest accomplishments. It will celebrate you and the epic adventure that is your life.

What scenes will you include? Which characters will join you? What moments and experiences will you show audiences in your movie?

Your answers to all of these questions, and the answers you wrote down above, make up your "Legacy Bucket List." Complete it on the next few pages. Include all of those things you want to do before you die, all of those places you want to visit and people you want to see. Include the experiences you want to have, things you want to learn and legacies you want to leave behind.

Find Your Future Self and start becoming it today so that you leave behind a legacy that is worthy of your life.

Finding Your Future Self
ACTIONS TO TAKE

1. Make a list of those things you want to do or experience in life, or the legacy you want to leave behind.

My Legacy Bucket List includes:

_____

_____

_____

_____

_____

_____

_____

_____

_____

_____

_____

_____

_____

_____

_____

_____

_____

_____

2. Write out what steps you have to take in order to begin moving towards each one of these goals, and as you proceed, add in other steps as they occur to you.

One Item from My Legacy Bucket List is:

_____

_____

Steps I will take on it:

_____

_____

_____

_____

_____

_____

Another Item from My Legacy Bucket List is:

_____

_____

Steps I will take on it:

_____

_____

_____

_____

_____

_____

Another Item from My Legacy Bucket List is:

_____

_____

Steps I will take on it:

_____

_____

_____

_____

Another Item from My Legacy Bucket List is:

_____

_____

Steps I will take on it:

_____

_____

_____

_____

(to be continued by you with other items from your list)

3. Take action on these steps so that you are moving in the direction of your goal.

14 | FIND YOUR SELF WITH A GUIDE

A guide is usually someone who has been there before or someone who knows how to navigate the territory you are about to enter. Sometimes a book like this one, or a map, can be a guide. It can give you direction, suggest strategies and how to avoid danger.

At other times you need a real person to guide you on your quest. Someone who can share the journey with you, someone you can ask questions of, someone who can help you adapt your approach along the way.

As a Life Coach that's exactly what I do. I help guide people through their lives. They are the ones in charge of the quest. It is their journey. I am simply there to help them and guide them in the directions they choose to go.

A coach and an athlete have the same relationship. As a coach, I am not the one out on the playing field, performing and competing in the game. You are. It's your game. You are the star player. Instead, I am on the sidelines, cheering you on, helping you to train in practice and review past performances to improve next time.

As a life coach I am just like a wilderness guide. I have travelled this territory before and can help you find your own best way to your dreams and desires.

Clients come to me for many reasons. If any of these sound familiar, coaching might be the right path for you to take out of this wilderness and I may be the right guide.

Some people come to work with me in order to heal from some sort of trauma or emotional pain. Perhaps you have suffered a divorce, lost a loved one, or just or recently left a bad relationship, suffered a financial loss, or need to get over childhood trauma. If this is the wilderness you face, then rest easy and know I have guided many travelers thought it before and I have crossed those dark plains myself.

Some people come to coaching in order to get over a destructive pattern, like dealing with depression, anger or addiction. Perhaps there is some pattern you keep repeating which has caused you many problems in the past and you're ready to be free from this cycle. If this is the wilderness you are lost in, have hope because I have guided many people, and found my own way, out of these dark caverns of despair and out into the light of freedom.

Some individuals come to me for help in achieving a goal or dream. Perhaps you want to start or grow a business, change careers, lose weight, write a book, or motivate your self to accomplish some other goal or achievement. If this is the mountain you intend to climb, put on your boots and get ready because I have led many people on their climb to the peak of achievement, just as I have climbed it myself and enjoyed its wonderful views.

Some people request my coaching in order to heal or improve a relationship. Perhaps you want to get more joy out of your romantic relationship, or you want to improve things with your kids or parents, or perhaps you want to be a better teacher or salesperson. If so, get ready to join the team, because I have guided many clients thought the process of improving relationships with those we are traveling through space and time with, and I have learned how to do this for myself.

Some people come to coaching in order to answer a question or make a difficult decision. Perhaps you aren't sure what to do about a particular issue in life. Perhaps you are weighing career options, or don't know whether couples counseling or divorce is best for you, or what to do with the next chapter of your life.

Some people see me to develop new skills. Perhaps you want to learn hypnosis, Neuro-Linguistic Programming, magic, sales strategies, or how to alleviate physical pain and speed healing.

Some people come to be guided in how to leave behind that which no longer serves them. Perhaps you need to find the courage and a way to leave an unhappy marriage, or unfulfilling job.

FIELD NOTES

Once you change your thinking, you change your self, and then you change your world.

Thoughts create Feelings. Feelings create Actions. Actions create Results.

I encourage you to contact me to explore if I am the right guide for you.

Although each person I work with comes to me for their own unique reasons and with their own unique experiences, histories and perspectives, all of them go through the same wonderful process. I help them find their way out of the darkness by gaining clarity on what they want and how to achieve it. Then, with my guidance, they climb that mountain and get to feast on the fruits of their success.

For me, the greatest experience in being a Life Coach, or guide, in this way is getting to watch my clients succeed and feel better than they ever imagined possible before. There is nothing like watching someone's thinking transform and the light that sparkles in their eyes as that epiphany dawns on them, and then they go out into the wild world and make that dream come true.

Peak experiences are wonderful and many people would say that they are rare in life. But I have had many, and every day I get to see the people I work with climb their own mountains and have their own peak experiences, as they look down on the world from above and watch their dreams and desires unfold before them. So, if seeing is believing, then I believe that we can have many, many peak experiences in life, especially because I see myself and others having them all the time.

If there is something you want in your life, or don't want any more in your life, I encourage you to contact me to explore if I am the right guide for you.

If there is something you want for your self, or don't want any more for your self, I urge you to contact me to discover for your self, if I can help you find your path.

Whether you choose to contact me or not, my best advice to you is to find a counselor or coach that feels right to you. Only you can know who the right one is for you. So take some time and explore a few different directions or guides and then settle on the one that speaks your language and touches your heart. This will be the right guide for you.

Visit me and www.MBMCoach.com or email me at MBMCoach2018@gmail.com, to see if I might be the right guide for this part of your journey.

As a Life Coach and a practitioner of Neuro-Linguistic Programming and hypnotherapy one of the things I help clients with the most is how to change their thinking.

Perhaps that doesn't sound very dramatic at first, but I can assure you it is. Once you change your thinking, you change your self, and then you change your world.

Like most mathematical formulas this truth is both simple and powerful. It is so elegant that it can be expressed in this way:

$$T \rightarrow F \rightarrow A \rightarrow R$$

This equation is so powerful that it explains how everything is manifested into physical reality and how you can literally change your entire world.

I call it the "Too Far Equation" because if you don't understand it, you're not going to go too far in life.

What it tells us is this:

Thoughts create Feelings. Feelings create Actions. Actions create Results.

Our thoughts, how we view things, our perceptions and our perspective, dictate how we feel about things. Whether something is good or bad, pleasant or unpleasant, is determined by how we think about it. So, how we think about it determines how we feel about it. Or, in more scientific terms, our thinking determines our neurochemistry.

Our neurochemistry or feelings are the emotions that put us into motion and cause us to take action. Our actions then get us the results that we receive from the world.

So, if we don't like the results we are getting, we need to back up and change our actions. If we don't like the way we are behaving, then we need to back up and change how we feel. If we don't like how we feel, then we need to back up and change our thinking. Everything starts on the inside. Everything that exists in the world started on the inside of someone's mind as a thought. And every change that a person makes in their life, from the greatest to the smallest, started out as a change in their thinking.

The greatest changes and most magical transformations people make are often invisible at first.

The greatest insights and life changing epiphanies cannot be seen at the moment they happen.

The change happens on the inside. You can't see it from outside. But on the inside, a thought has changed, a perception has shifted, and for that person all of a sudden the world has changed forever.

From the outside they look the same, but they have been powerfully changed, and nothing will ever be the same again, and they know it, and this makes them feel very happy, free and strong.

The person looks the same. Their outward life seems the same, for now, yet somehow, they have completely changed on the inside and they know it. They also know that change always happens on the inside first, then it happens on the outside.

They suddenly feel so relieved and happy that the change they wanted is coming that a smile spreads across their face. They lift their head up higher, their eyes ignite with fire, and you can begin to see it. Even from the outside, you can begin to see it happening.

Change is coming. Change is here.

Now, even from the outside you can see it. They have changed and soon everything around them will change.

I've watched this change happen many times with my clients. I've experienced this change many times myself. I've listened to my clients talk about how this change felt and what it meant in their lives and I've reflected on its importance and affect myself. From all of these lived experiences, I can tell you that the most powerful thing in the universe is a changed mind, and it's invisible to the outsider. But the insider understands the power and significance of this change.

One minute everything is hopeless: they are the powerless victim and nothing is working out for them. The next moment, without any change in the external physical reality of their life, everything is different. Everything is better. Now, they are the creator of their own reality, the master of their destiny, and they know everything will work out for them: They are filled with hope and carried on its wings.

I've observed my clients closely, many times, at this moment of transformation, and if you look and listen and feel carefully enough, you can see if from the outside. The head uplifts. The eyes brighten.

Nostrils dilate. Chest comes out, shoulders go back. There is a positive and confident inflection in their tone of voice and a shift in the volume and pace. Their energy pulsates outward pushing at you instead of pulling and sucking in.

You will hear them say "I get it now. It's all different."

You will see the relief and joy and confidence in their face and you know that even though they haven't had a chance to make those outward changes yet, everything really is different. Everything has already begun to change.

Now they are going to leave that abusive partner or unfulfilling job.

Now they are going to start that business or join that class.

Now they are going to get sober or in shape, or start sleeping at night, or stop yelling at their kids.

Now if you look close you can see it and if you listen hard and feel soft you can hear and feel it.

They have changed.

There is a different person sitting in front of you now and that person is going to behave differently and get different results from the world.

They know it.

You know it.

You both know that their mind has changed, their perspective, their perception has changed, and thus their experience of reality will change.

They have changed neuro-chemically and energetically. They are vibrating on a different frequency now, vibrating at a different pace and speed. Because their energetic vibrations have changed and because we are all nothing but energy at the subatomic level, they have completely changed and their life is about to change completely.

All this has happened, is happening, and will happen for you once you have succeeded in changing their thinking.

Change your thinking, change your self.

Change your self, change your world.

As you engage in this process you may want a guide to help you learn how to change your thinking. If so, give me a call and I'll come to aid you on your journey. Also know that I am not the only guide. There are many here on this planet for you. So, rest easy my friend, you don't have to walk the path all alone.

Finding Your Self with a Guide
ACTIONS TO TAKE

1. Visit me, MindBody Master Dr. Corey Lewis, online at www. MBMCoach.com Look at the resources I have developed there and contact me to see if my approach is a good fit for you at MBMCoach2018@gmail.com

If I could get anything out of Coaching with Corey, this is what I would want:

_____

_____

_____

_____

_____

_____

_____

_____

_____

_____

_____

_____

_____

_____

2. Research other coaches, teachers, counselors or therapists who may be able to guide you on your own unique journey.

Others who can help guide me:

_____

_____

_____

_____

_____

_____

_____

_____

_____

_____

_____

_____

_____

_____

_____

_____

_____

_____

_____

_____

15 | MAP YOUR MANY SELVES

When I began leading groups in backcountry wilderness areas, we didn't have GPS. We learned the traditional way of using a map and orienting it by landmarks or by compass. We learned to memorize landscapes and count ridges and drainages until it became habit. Later, with the advent of technology, many of my students began showing up with GPS units, and most often, at some point during the trip their units failed. Either the batteries died, or maps failed to load, or it got wet or broken, or whatever, they often didn't function. So, I always required that my students learn how to use a map and compass the old school way.

One of the best things about using a map is that you begin to learn and memorize the entire landscape. This is what we mean by "getting the lay of the land." It means learning how the landforms around you are laid down, where the ridges and rivers are, where the forests and meadows are, and so on.

So, if you are lost and want to Find Your Self, you need a good map of the territory. A good map will help you know what direction you want to go in, how to get there, and what obstacles you will face along the way. If the wilderness you are lost in happens to be your life, then you need a good map of your life and your self in order to find your way.

A Life Map will give you a direction to go in life and show you how to get there in exactly the same way that a map can show you where to go in the wilderness.

Just in case you aren't familiar with land navigation in the wilderness, here are the basics of how you use a map and compass. You take your compass and find north and you orient your map so that north on the paper is north in the real world. Then you look from the map to the real world around you, back and forth, and identify each hill, edge of forest, stream, landmark and so on, until you know where you are and where everything else is.

Then, once you have determined where you are, you find the spot on the map you want to go to, and you take a bearing with your compass between the two. A bearing shows you on your compass the exact direction you need to go, in order to hit your chosen spot. It might tell you, for example, that you must go 40 degrees northeast, or 240 degrees southwest, to hit your chosen spot, and then you don't have to look at the map anymore. You fold it up and look only at your compass to make sure you stay on the same bearing, until you reach your goal.

So, you use your map to determine your location and destination, where you are now and where you want to be in six months or a year. And, you use your compass to determine your bearing, what direction you need to go and the steps you need to take along the way to reach your goal.

In this exercise you are going to create a map of all your different selves and your favorite things to do for each self. Then, when you choose to go in one direction, toward a specific self, you will take a compass bearing by listing all the steps you can think of, or landmarks you will see, along the way. Then follow that bearing and find that facet of Your Self.

So, let us get down to the business of mapping the landscape of Your Many Selves.

I've provided a map for you on the following pages that you can use to Map your favorite activities and ideas for each of your many selves that you explored in this book. I have also provided an 11x17 inch downloadable map that you can fill out online or print out at MBMCoach.com.

As you will see on the Map of Your Many Selves there are 12 Circles, one representing each of your different selves. Your Present Self and Next Self are near the center of the map, while your Past Self is on the left and your Future Self is on the right. Above and below this are all of your other selves.

In order to Map Your Many Selves, fill in each circle with your favorite ideas and activities for that self, from that chapter of this book. You might simply write these ideas down in the circle or add symbols or pictures that visually represent those things.

1. Map Your Present Self
2. Map Your Next Self
3. Map Your Past Self
4. Map Your Future Self
5. Map Your Fun Self
6. Map Your Natural Self
7. Map Your Spiritual Self
8. Map Your Physical Self
9. Map Your Better Self
10. Map Your New Self
11. Map Your Self Alone
12. Map Your Self Among Others

After you Map these Different Selves, add in lines connecting Different Selves to each other if they are achieved in similar ways, or are mutually reinforcing, and so on.

For example, perhaps eating healthier and running on a regular basis are both goals for your New Self and your Physical Self and your Future Self. You also notice that quitting smoking, part of your Better Self, is connected to this healthier lifestyle. In addition, you remember that your friend Marci is a great, healthy cook and you could get together with her once each week to cook a meal together, and that your friend Joe runs regularly and you could go at least once a week with him. A final benefit is that both Marci and Joe are on your Find Your Self Among Others and your Find Your Fun Self lists.

By drawing these lines of connection, your map will show you which activities are mutually reinforcing. They take you in the same direction and fulfill different purposes, or fulfill different Selves, at one and the same time. You might also want to color code activities that are connected to each other.

The more interconnected you can make your activities, meaning the more Selves they satisfy at once, the more pleasure and benefit you will get from them and the easier they will be to do.

I want you to know that you are unique and valuable. You are a rare gem. You are like a diamond with many different facets, each one shining in its own brilliance. Take the time to polish up and enjoy each facet of your self, and then...

Shine my friend.

Shine like the diamond you are!

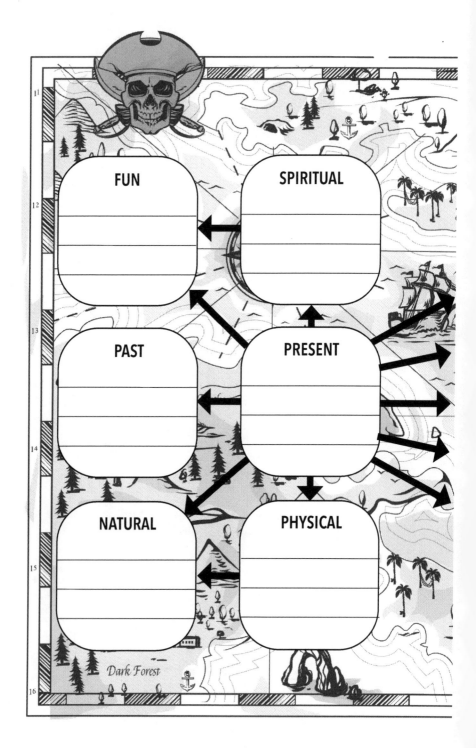

FUN

SPIRITUAL

PAST

PRESENT

NATURAL

PHYSICAL

Dark Forest

142

Map of Your Many Selves

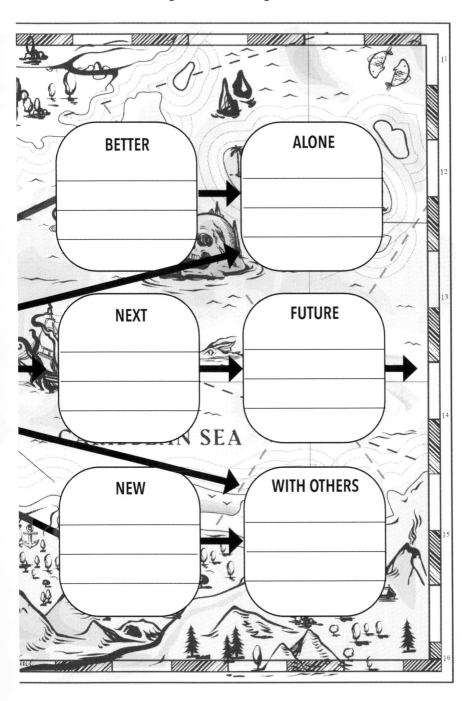

Mapping Your Many Selves
ACTIONS TO TAKE

1. Make a visual map that contains items from each chapter in this book of your many selves. (Past, present, future, alone, among others, and so on). Use the blank map provided in this chapter, or download the larger, 11x17 inch, map from MBMCoach.com.

2. Connect related or overlapping items in some visual way, with either similar colors or connecting lines. Take note of which activities fulfill different parts of your self at the same time.

3. Put your map up where you can see it every day. Then, decide on an item, or items, to pursue and list the steps you need to take to get there, and then take action. Listing out these steps—making a plan for what you will do, which direction you will go in—is how you take a compass bearing off of your map. Then, take action by following that compass bearing, or plan, until you reach your destination.

Then, take action by following that compass bearing, or plan, until you reach your destination.

16 | TAKE ACTION WITH YOURSELF

Congratulations! You have read the book. But, have you done anything yet?

Until you make a change, nothing changes.

It is the difference that makes a difference.

You are what you do, not what you intend or pretend to do.

You're worth the effort of taking action and your life is worth taking action for and nothing will change if you don't change it.

If you don't do anything different, then ten years from now you will still feel lost, and you will have lost thousands of days on inaction and thousands of dollars on self-help books and videos without ever enjoying any improvements in your life. I know you don't want that. You found this book, or it found you, for a reason. You want to take action on the ideas in this book and you want to enjoy your self and your life as fully as possible. That's why you read the book. But reading and knowing isn't enough. You must apply what you know. You must take action on what you read.

Nothing happens until you make it happen. So, in order to get what you want you must take action.

If you haven't take action yet, you can start taking action in one of two ways:

1) Start at the beginning of the *Field Guide to Finding Your Self* and skim the first chapter and do the exercises at the end of that chapter immediately. Then, take at least one action on those exercises, before reading the next chapter. Then, skim the second chapter, complete the exercises, and take at least one action on them before you go to the next chapter.

2) If that's too daunting, pick one chapter, any chapter, whichever one you are the most drawn to, and do the exercises in it, and take action on those exercises before going to any other chapters. Then, pick another easy chapter to do, and complete those exercises and take action on them. As you continue this process, it will get easier for you to take action, even on those chapters that seemed especially difficult for you at first.

Once you begin taking action, you will begin to build momentum and everything will snowball from there, one action leading to others and those leading to many other actions.

It is important in life to understand the power of both inertia and momentum, especially if you want to make a change or make anything happen.

Inertia is the tendency of an object at rest to stay at rest. Momentum is the tendency of a moving object to keep moving. Imagine a freight train sitting still on the tracks. It has hundreds of cars, each weighing thousands of pounds. It takes a tremendous amount of energy just to get that train moving. In fact, it takes more energy to get that train to go from zero to one mile per hour than it does to get that train to go from 20 to 40 miles per hour. That is the power of inertia.

Now imagine that same train barreling down the track at 80 miles per hour. Imagine how much energy it takes to stop that train or even slow it down. In fact, it takes more energy to slow that train down from 80 miles per hour to 60, then it does to speed it up to 100 miles per hour. That is the power of momentum.

If you want your life to move, or if you want to move through your life, instead of just sitting still, you need to be able to break inertia and build momentum.

In psychological terms we often recognize the power of inertia as the procrastination barrier. These are the obstacles that prevent you from getting started and taking action. They consist of thoughts like "It doesn't matter whether I do it or not." "It won't make any difference anyway." "It probably won't work for me." "It takes too much effort and is too difficult." "I'll get started on it later, or tomorrow, or next week."

In order to break inertia, you just have to get the train rolling, a little bit. Get it moving just a few inches, and then it will continue to roll a few feet more, and soon you're steaming down the track.

In order to break the procrastination barrier, you just have to change your thoughts and take the smallest of actions. Replace those negative thoughts with something like "It does matter, and it will work, and the effort is worth it, and I'm going to start right now, with the easiest action I can think of first." Then take that tiny action and feel your self begin to move, and you will continue to roll forward onto the next action, and the next, until you have become a charging locomotive barreling down the track of life!

The reason this book came to you is because:

    You want to experience your best self imaginable.

    You want to express your best self imaginable.

    You want to live the best life imaginable.

And when you take action on what you write down in this book and in your journal, you will.

And if you don't, you won't.

Remember, right now the rest of your life is on the line. Save your self. Save your life.

You are the hero you have been waiting for!

So, when would now be a good time to start?

ABOUT THE AUTHOR

Dr. Corey Lewis is a personal and professional development coach, author and speaker. Corey spent many years working with backcountry trail, forestry and research crews with the Nevada Conservation Corps, USFS, and a variety of different Universities. His first book, *Reading the Trail*, discusses the benefits of engaging students in experientially-based and holistic forms of education. Master Lewis is a 7th Dan Black Belt in Taekwondo, former national champion, and owner of Sun Yi's Academy of Taekwondo in Arcata, California. As founder of MindBody Mastery, Corey has coached many people through the process of finding themselves and their purpose in life, so that they can live the life of their dreams. Dr. Lewis combines a number of powerful modalities to help clients ranging from Neuro-Linguistic Programming and Hypnotherapy, to Cognitive Psychology, Reiki, Meditation, Nutrition, Biofeedback, and more.

Visit www.MBMCoach.com to find out more about MindBody Master Corey Lewis and the wide variety of resources available for you there.

facebook.com/mindbodymastery
youtube.com/channel/UCYfLqV4yOiKdx-nQmrByO9w

Supercharge Your Experience with the Who Am I? Hypnotic Induction

at www.MBMCoach.com
mbmcoach.com/product/who-am-i-hypnotic-trance-induction/

Who am I? Why am I here? Where am I going? What is my purpose? These are some of the most profound questions in life and when we answer them well, we get a life that is truly fulfilling.

This one-of-a-kind Hypnotic Induction will help bring you into a deep trance at Alpha brain wave levels where you can explore your answers to these questions and gain clarity on what you want to Be, Do, and Have in life, and Why.

As Dr. Lewis guides you through reviewing your past experiences, passions and feelings, you will gain a clear and powerful sense of who you are, what your purpose on this planet is, and how you want to experience and express that best self!

If you have never experienced Hypnosis before, you can start getting curious and prepare for a truly wonderful experience. If you are concerned about hypnosis, you needn't worry; Another way to describe a Hypnotic Induction is simply as a Guided Meditation. In both cases, your guide, Dr. Lewis, helps you relax your mind from Beta brain wave levels, our waking state, to Alpha, that meditative state we go to just on the edge of sleep. In this heightened state of consciousness, you gain greater clarity, have more creativity, and can program your mind directly to help you do, whatever it is you want to do.

By now I hope you are ready to uncover who you really are with clarity and conviction so that you can experience your best self and live life like never before!

OTHER BOOKS AND RESOURCES

From MindBody Master Dr. Corey Lee Lewis
www.MBMCoach.com

BOOKS

Visit your local bookstore, online bookseller,
Amazon.com or Abebooks.com to get your copy today.

The Art of Becoming: Quantum Leaping into Your Future Self.

amazon.com/Art-Becoming-Quantum-Leaping-Future-ebook/dp/
B07964XFW8/

This one-of-a-kind story is part epic adventure and part instruction
manual. After suffering a divorce and the death of two loved ones,
Dr. Lewis began Quantum Leaping into the future to heal his pain
and learn from his future self. You will follow MindBody Master
Dr. Corey Lewis as he develops his method of Quantum Leaping
into the future and you will learn how to practice the technique
yourself. You can follow him on these adventures and you will learn
the techniques for personal transformation that he learned and
developed along the way. Readers have said "I couldn't put the book
down." "It's exactly what I need right now in my life." And "The story
was so engaging I couldn't stop reading." If you would like Dr. Lewis
to lead you on your own Quantum Leap check out the Hypnotic
Induction in the "Resources" section of this book.

The Dream Machine Workbook

amazon.com/Dream-Machine-Workbook-Corey-Lewis/
dp/1671913981/

The ability to take a dream and turn it into a creative process is
what separates mere dreamers from those who achieve the life of
their dreams. The Dream Machine Workbook will lead you through,
and teach you this process, so that you can manifest any dream you
want for the rest of your life.

This Workbook will take you through each step in the Dreaming
and Planning Process to achieve the life of your dreams in all 8
categories of life: emotionally, physically, spiritually, family life,

social life, love life, career/finances, experiences/things. You will be taught how to dream bigger than ever before, and then you will be taken through a strategic planning process that turns those giant dreams into smaller goals, and actionable steps that can be taken today to move you toward your dreams. You will learn how to break the procrastination barrier, manage your time, enhance your motivation, and more, until your wildest dreams are part of your daily reality! If you would like Dr. Lewis to guide you through this process and help you complete the workbook, check out The Dream Machine Class Series in the "Resources" section of this book.

Sleep Now: Bedtime Stories to Help Your Kids Go to Sleep

amazon.com/Sleep-Now-Bedtime-Stories-Children/dp/B084P575C6/

This extremely helpful book will make the difficulties of bedtime a thing of the past. Each story takes your child on an imaginative and relaxing journey while using hypnotic commands and language patterns to relax them and make them fall asleep. Simply by reading these stories out loud to your children, you will be turned into a masterful hypnotist who can easily get your children to fall asleep every night. Each night you can take them on a different adventure—to magic dragon land, or the undersea world, or a winter wonderland, or the land of dinosaurs, and more—all while helping them to relax and fall asleep.

You can download a recording of Dr. Lewis, the master hypnotist himself, reading one of the stories from *Sleep Now* to play your children and to learn the techniques for yourself at www. MBMCoach.com, and if you have difficulty sleeping, yourself, check out the "Sleep Well" Hypnotic Induction in the "Resources" section of this book.

Life Lessons from a Martial Arts Master

amazon.com/Life-Lessons-Martial-Arts-Master/dp/B08GFTLK6G/

The image of the Martial Arts Master teaching students much more than physical techniques, the guru also teaching life lessons, is so common in film and literature because it is so true in Martial Arts tradition and current practice. The Martial Arts provide a "Path" or "Way," literally translated as "Do," for how to live your life in harmony and balance, how to live happily with health and success. In *Life Lessons from a Martial Arts Master*, 7th Dan Black Belt, Taekwondo Master and tenured Professor, Dr. Corey Lewis distills a lifetime of Martial Arts practice down into twenty-one life lessons that you can apply to any area of your life, both on and off the mat. Whether you are a Martial Arts Instructor, student or fan, or even if you know nothing of the Martial Arts, this book will provide you with twenty-one life changing lessons and guide you through putting those exercises into action. As Bruce Lee said "Knowing is not enough, we must apply. Willing is not enough, we must do."

Life Lessons from a Martial Arts Master Workbook

amazon.com/Life-Lessons-Martial-Master-Workbook/dp/
B08QLQHGKQ/

This Workbook is designed to work on its own, or as a supplement to *Life Lessons from a Martial Arts Master*. In this Workbook you will be given the space, and guided through the process, of putting each of the Life Lessons into practice. Put each of these twenty-one powerful principles into action and enjoy watching your life transform for the better.

RESOURCES

For Free Class Modules, Guided Meditations, Video Classes, and more...
Visit www.MBMCoach.com

Or, the MindBody Mastery Channel on Youtube
youtube.com/channel/UCYfLqV4yOiKdx-nQmrByO9w

Free Headache and Migraine Cure Video

mbmcoach2018-e87fa.gr8.com/

Would you like to be able to cure any headache within minutes, without any medication or side effects?

In this Free Video I will teach you how to cure migraines and headaches in just a few minutes using a powerful method that I developed which combines Neuro-Linguistic Programming, Biofeedback, Acupressure, and Hypnosis. You can use this powerful technique to cure your own headaches, or others, so that you, and your loved ones, can be pain free for life.

Free Daily Power Habits PDF Class Module

mbmcoach.com/product/daily-power-habits/

This Free Class Module will teach you the Seven Daily Strategies for Emotional Alignment and Success that you can use to enhance your feelings of happiness, gratitude and motivation on a daily basis, so that you feel better and get better results out of yourself and the world. Every single one of Dr. Lewis's coaching clients, whether they are working on personal or professional development, begin their work with these Daily Power Habits. Learn how to use them now to enjoy your life more in the present and improve it in the future.

Free Relax Now PDF Class Module

mbmcoach.com/product/relax-now-class-module-1/

Many of us suffer from high levels of stress and anxiety in today's fast-paced, uncertain world. Would you like to know how to reduce stress, avoid panic attacks, and become more emotionally aligned and happy than before?

This Free Class Module will teach you a variety of methods for reducing your stress and problems with anxiety and fear ranging from how to balance your neuro-chemistry with exercise, meditation and specific vitamins and supplements, to how to deal with these negative emotions in the moment when they arise. For more information on this topic check out the "Relax Now Video Class" and "Relax Now Hypnotic Induction" onMBM.Coach.com

Free Video: Set an Anchor for Joy and Optimism

youtube.com/watch?v=ECdq6IkVYKo

This Free Video, which is available on the MindBody Mastery Youtube channel, will help you sett an anchor, or trigger, for joy

154

and optimism that you can fire off anytime you want in order to feel happier, and more hopeful, about life. If you want to feel good for no reason at all, then watch this video.

Free Video: Learn Biofeedback to Raise Your Body's Temperature

youtube.com/watch?v=qVrqwWy3TeA

In this Free Video, which is available on the MindBody Mastery Youtube channel, you will learn how to use Biofeedback in order to control your blood flow, and raise or lower the temperature of various parts of your body. Learning this foundational Biofeedback technique will help you perform other mind over body feats, such as lowering your blood pressure, reducing pain, and speeding healing, and more.

The Dream Machine Class Series

mbmcoach.com/product/the-dream-machine-class-series/

The ability to take a dream and turn it into a creative process is what separates mere dreamers from those who achieve the life of their dreams. The Dream Machine Class Series will lead you through, and teach you this process, so that you can manifest any dream for the rest of your life.

This Class Series will take you through each step in the Dreaming and Planning Process to achieve the life of your dreams in all 8 categories of life: emotionally, physically, spiritually, family life, social life, love life, career/finances, experiences/things.

Each of the three 90-minute video classes will guide you through the Dream Machine Planning process as well as motivate you like never before with their already included trance inductions. You will learn how to dream bigger than ever before, and how to turn those dreams into feasible goals and actionable steps you can take today. You will learn how to break the procrastination barrier, manage time, and motivate yourself like never before. I recommend that you also purchase the Dream Machine Workbook to work through as you take the classes.

Samurai Strategies for Success: How to Survive and Thrive in Tumultuous Times

mbmcoach.com/product/samurai-strategies-for-success/

This Video Class Series is made up of Three, 1-Hour Long, recordings of Webinar Classes Dr. Lewis has led other MindBody Mastery students through.

These classes have been designed specifically to help you adapt both personally and professionally to the radical changes we are experiencing during this pandemic, or to any changes or transitions you face in life. *Class One: Maintaining Your Emotional Alignment. Class Two: Clarifying Your Personal Life Purpose. Class Three: Adapting Yourself Professionally.*

Each class has corresponding homework for you to complete, as you learn how to apply the principles from class to your everyday life. Soon, you will see obstacles as opportunities and change will become your chance to make all your dreams come true!

Sleep Well Hypnotic Trance Induction

mbmcoach.com/product/sleep-well-hypnotic-trance-induction/

Do you have trouble falling asleep or staying asleep throughout the night?

This Sleep Well Hypnotic Induction will help you relax both your mind and body deeply, lower your heart rate and brain wave activity, and help you slip easily into a gentle slumber each night when you got to bed. In addition, it will also help program your mind to stay relaxed and sleep deeply the whole night through, so that you wake up refreshed, energized and ready for your day.

By listening to this Induction each night when you go to bed, you can train yourself to use these relaxation techniques on your own, so that you will be able to train yourself to fall asleep easily and stay asleep all night long, on your own, for the rest of your life. Get ready now to make insomnia a thing in your past and to sleep better than ever before!

If You have children who have difficulty going to sleep, check out my book *Sleep Now: Bedtime Stories to Help Your Children Go to Sleep*. These stories will entertain and relax your children helping them to fall asleep easier than ever.

Quantum Leap into Your Future Hypnotic Trance Induction

mbmcoach.com/product/sleep-well-hypnotic-trance-induction/

What if you could jump forward into the future, over the obstacles you face now and bring back with you, the solutions you need in the present?

If you are interested in learning MindBody Master Corey Lewis's Quantum Leaping technique, this guided meditation will show you how. In *The Art of Becoming: Quantum Leaping into Your Future Self* Dr. Lewis describes how he developed the technique to overcome the pain of a divorce and the death of two loved ones, a technique you can learn now.

This audio-recording can be listened to once, or multiple times, and will bring you to Alpha Brain Wave Levels so that you can powerfully connect with your future self. During this Hypnotic induction MindBody Master Dr. Lewis will lead you through your Quantum Leap so that you can successfully bring back the insights and resources you need now to make that future become your present reality.

Improve Your Athletic Performance Hypnotic Trance Induction

mbmcoach.com/product/sports-performance-induction/

In this Sports Performance Induction, Dr. Lewis will guide you through using Mental Rehearsal to train your neurophysiology to perform flawlessly, just as you use Physical Practice to train your muscles to perform correctly. This process is called "Visual Motor Rehearsal" and is used by all of our Olympic and most of our professional teams. Dr. Lewis has helped thousands of athletes improve their performance with this method, ranging from Olympians and Professional Athletes to amateurs and children.

I will guide you through a series of scenes where you will see and feel yourself performing flawlessly and succeeding wonderfully so that you are psychologically and physiologically primed to get the best performance out of yourself ever. I will also help you create a "Highlight Reel" that you can quickly re-play in your mind, anytime you want, in order to get that surge of confidence you need to be your best. In addition, after you have listened to, and practiced, this Sports Performance Guided Meditation a few times, you will be able to do it on your own, anytime you want.

Hungry Like a Lion Hypnotic Trance Induction

mbmcoach.com/product/hungry-like-a-lion-hypnotic-trance-induction/

Whatever your dream, desire or goal, you need to be powerfully motivated to take action if you want to achieve it. This powerful Hypnotic Induction will build in you the desire and motivation to stalk and hunt down your goals tirelessly like a hungry lion. This audio-recording can be listened to once, or multiple times, and will bring you to Alpha Brain Wave Levels so that you can powerfully program your conscious and unconscious mind to work for you. Get the motivation you need to break the procrastination barrier and begin building the momentum that will propel you toward achieving your goals with this Guided Meditation.

Chakra Alignment Hypnotic Trance Induction

mbmcoach.com/product/chakra-alignment-hypnotic-trance-induction/

This powerful guided meditation will teach you how to center yourself and align your energetic chakras to bring you back into balance and feel better than ever before. Have you ever wanted to feel that Kundalini energy flying up your spine and your own Chi building in your body? With this powerful technique, you will. Do you ever feel pushed out of balance, or like you are scattered in too many directions? This guided meditation will teach you how to center and ground yourself so that you feel focused and clear and ready to take on life's many challenges.

OTHER BOOKS
BY DR. COREY LEE LEWIS

Reading the Trail: Exploring the Literature and
Natural History of the California Crest

The Pacific Crest Trailside Readers:
Volume I California.
Volume II Oregon/Washington

The Art of Becoming: Quantum Leaping into Your Future Self

Sleep Now: Bedtime Stories to Help Your Children Go to Sleep

The Dream Machine Workbook

Life Lessons from a Martial Arts Master

Life Lessons from a Martial Arts Master Workbook

Made in the USA
Columbia, SC
29 July 2024